ISO 9000-3

Springer
New York
Berlin
Heidelberg
Barcelona
Budapest
Hong Kong
London
Milan
Paris
Santa Clara
Singapore
Tokyo

Raymond Kehoe   Alka Jarvis

ISO 9000-3

A Tool for Software Product and Process Improvement

Springer

Raymond Kehoe
1358 Suzanne Court
San Jose, CA 95129
USA

Alka Jarvis
978 Addison Avenue
Palo Alto, CA 94301
USA

On the cover: An illustration of the business of software development.

With 2 figures.

Library of Congress Cataloging-in-Publication Data
Kehoe, Ray.
    ISO 9000-3: a tool for software product and process improvement/
Ray Kehoe, Alka Jarvis.
        p. cm.
    Includes bibliographical references and index.
    ISBN 0-387-94568-7 (hardcover: alk. paper)
    1. Computer software — Quality control.   I. Jarvis, Alka.
    II. Title.
    QA76.76.Q35K44   1995
    005.1′068′5 — dc20   95-30506

Printed on acid-free paper.

Production managed by Francine McNeill; manufacturing supervised by Jeffrey Taub.
Typeset in LaTeX using the authors' Microsoft Word files.
Printed and bound by R.R. Donnelley and Sons, Harrisonburg, VA.
Printed in the United States of America.

9 8 7 6 5 4 3 2 1

ISBN 0-387-94568-7 Springer-Verlag New York Berlin Heidelberg

Alka: To my husband, Steve, and my parents, Bansilal and Prabha Parikh, for their support and encouragement.

Ray: To Mom, Dad, Denise, and three little wolfies.

Acknowledgments

The authors want to thank their many friends and colleagues who gave helpful feedback on the contents of this book. We are grateful to the following individuals: Karen Snow, Estella Weems, Joe Blank, Brad "Princeton" Houser, Georgi Brisker, Madhvi Pratt, Mark Gustoff, Cary Schneider, Jeff Schlageter, Chuck Steele, and J.R. Rutledge. Special thanks to Harry Max, an exceptional technical writer.

We would especially like to thank Tim Johnson, Sharon Omori, and Virginia Sanchez of the University of Santa Cruz Extension Program, whose vision and hard work in creating the Extension Program has provided us the opportunity to develop the course that this book is based on. Finally, we wish to acknowledge our editor, Martin Gilchrist, whose patience has been most appreciated.

Contents

Introduction

Purpose

The purpose of this book is to provide the reader with an understanding of the ISO 9000-3 guideline and how it applies to the specification, development, test, and maintenance of software. We will show that the basic practices and procedures that define software engineering and the ISO guideline are, for all intents and purposes, one and the same. We hope that the readers of this book will use the information found within not only to pass the certification audit but as a tool to be used to create the well-managed engineering environment needed to create reliable, well-engineered products in a consistent manner.

Audience

This book is intended for senior software engineers, software managers, and non-software managers within software organizations whose aim is to create an engineering environment within their company or organization. In addition, individuals outside the software organization who have responsibility for the specification of the software product and preparing their organization to take ownership of the developed product will find this book of great interest. Finally, those who must choose software companies to do business with or audit software companies to determine their ability to engineer and maintain a software product will find this book helpful.

Overview

This book is made up of twenty-four chapters that can be grouped into four sections. Chapter 1 through Chapter 4 set the basis for the following chapters that deal directly with the guideline. These first four chapters describe the background of the ISO movement and provide an overview of software engineering. In addition we have included an overview of software engineering that will enable the reader to better understand the application of the guideline. We also hope that this overview will serve as a basis for discussion within the software organization, in that such discussion will lead to a single unified understanding of software engineering. A critical chapter is Chapter 3, in which we offer our interpretation and criticism of the guideline.

Chapter 5 through Chapter 8 address management responsibilities as identified in the guideline. These chapters focus on supplier management (software vendor) and purchaser management (software user) responsibilities involved in the specification of the product and the contract governing the work to be performed by both parties in the development and testing of the product. An especially important chapter is Chapter 7, which addresses the supplier management's responsibility for the creation and sustaining of an engineering environment in which the product is created and maintained. This primary responsibility is one that must be met if the supplier's organization is to create reliable products in a reliable, repeatable manner.

Chapter 9 through Chapter 13 discuss the activities involved in the planning, development, testing, and maintenance of the software product. The guideline is fairly general in its discussion of these topics and does not attempt to identify any particular development or maintenance life cycle. One activity that does receive the guideline's particular attention is purchaser acceptance of the product (Chapter 13). A major theme of the guideline is that the purchaser has explicit responsibilities that must be met, while the supplier, at the same time, must be ready to support the purchaser and respond to the purchaser's requests concerning the product during the acceptance process.

Chapter 14 through Chapter 19 discuss the activities that are used to manage the development and maintenance of a reliable product. Configuration management, documentation control, testing and management of third-party products, and a metric's program are all management activities used to ensure the reliability of a product. One last topic, training, receives only cursory attention in the guideline.

To increase the likelihood that an engineered product will meet the purchaser's needs, there should be explicitly, agreed-upon requirements and an engineering environment to turn those requirements into a product. Chapters 22 through 24 are provided to help the readers pass some of the basic hurdles in creating an engineering organization and identifying product requirements. Chapter 22 discusses how the purchaser and supplier (or marketing and engineering) can work together to identify product requirements. Chapter 23 provides an overview of configuration management, the process used to control product baselines. Chapter 24 presents a generic software process handbook that documents the basic steps in the development and maintenance of a software product.

1

Introduction to ISO 9000

The ISO standards were developed with the intent of creating a set of common standards for quality management and quality assurance. The standards can be applied to the manufacturing and service industries regardless of a company's size or the complexity of the product or service. The standards were developed by the International Organization for Standardization in Geneva, Switzerland. This organization was established in 1946 and has chapters in Germany (DIN), the United States (ANSI), France (AFNOR), and the United Kingdom (BSI).

These standards form the basis of an audit process that is performed by independent auditors. Much like accounting auditors, these quality auditors assure prospective customers that an audited company follows commonly accepted engineering practices and procedures in developing or manufacturing a product or providing a service. It is important to note that ISO 9000 does not guarantee quality products. The basic principle that the ISO 9000 program is based upon is that organizations that follow accepted practices and procedures are more likely to create reliable products in a consistent manner that meet the customer's needs than those organizations that do not follow accepted practices and procedures.

Since its publication in 1987, nearly 60 countries have adopted the standards, including the United States, Canada, Japan, and members of the European Community. Approximately 31,000 companies worldwide are certified to one of the series of ISO standards. Through the Institute of Electrical and Electronic Engineer's (IEEE's) technical advisory group, the United States contributes to the improvement of ISO 9000. ISO has five related components that are numbered from 9000 through 9004. These are listed below:

ISO 9000: Quality management and quality assurance standards: guideline for selection and use

ISO 9000-1: Revision of ISO 9000—1994

ISO 9000-3: guideline for application of ISO 9001 to the development, supply, and maintenance of software—1991

ISO 9001: Quality systems: Model for quality assurance in design/development, production, installation, and servicing—1994

ISO 9002: Quality systems: Model for quality assurance in production, installation, and servicing—1994

ISO 9003: Quality systems: Model for quality assurance in final inspection and test—1994

ISO 9004: Quality management and quality system elements—guideline—1987

ISO 9004-2: Quality management and quality system elements—Part 2: guideline for services—1991

The dates of the above are current as of this printing.

The requirements for a quality system between two parties have been established in ISO 9001; however, software development and maintenance is somewhat different from manufacturing or other industries in that software is very much a research and development effort as opposed to pure manufacturing or service. On the other hand, software is a product and software development is an engineering process. Software engineering has practices, principles, and procedures that are used to perform and control analysis, design, implementation, test, and maintenance of the software product.

ISO 9001 and ISO 9000-3

Due to the research and development aspects of software development, there is a greater need to coordinate the activities of the purchaser and the supplier to ensure that the product delivered is the product that is needed and that both the supplier and the purchaser are ready and able to fulfill their duties in the specification, development, installation, and support of that product. The ISO 9000-3 is an almost 100% expansion of the 9000-1 standard and was developed to provide guidelines for the application of ISO 9001 to the specification, development, installation, and support of software.

ISO 9001 "Shalls" and ISO 9000-3 "Shoulds"

The ISO 9000-3 guideline uses, in many of the sections, the word "should" when describing the process to be used by supplier or purchaser to ensure the quality of the product, while in several other sections (i.e., 4.1.1.2, 4.1.1.2.2, 4.1.1.2.3, 4.3, 6.2.4, 6.3, 6.7.2) the guideline uses the word "shall." Yet, in the IS0 9000-1 all the sections that the guideline is derived from use the word "shall." The difference between "shall" and "should" is that when "shall" is used, then a company must perform the practice associated with the word "shall." When "should" is used, then it is only recommended that a company perform that practice. Since the auditors will certify a company based on ISO 9000-1 and since all the sections in the guideline are derived from ISO 9000-1, we suggest that the reader should treat all the "shoulds" in the guideline as if they were "shalls."

2

Overview of
Software Engineering

This chapter is a high-level overview of software engineering and is meant to serve as an introduction for those who may not be familiar with, or only have a partial understanding of, software engineering. In addition, this overview can be useful to organizations that are trying to establish a common, organization-wide understanding of software engineering. Without such an understanding, many organizations will struggle to implement the engineering activities identified in the ISO 9000-3 guideline that, when all things are considered, are meant to aid in the development of reliable products in an expeditious manner.

This chapter also briefly discusses those product attributes, besides functionality, that have an impact on a product's quality and are often overlooked by many software development organizations during development and by customers during product specification.

For over twenty years, people in the software industry have been aware that there is a process for specifying, designing, implementing, and testing software that is based on engineering principles, practices, and accepted methodologies. And yet, even with knowledge of this process and the best intentions, new products continue to fail to meet a minimum criterion for sufficiency set forth by customers, investors, and even the designers themselves; that is, programmers and development teams rarely achieve their functional, technical, and reliability objectives, often missing schedule and cost targets.

In the past, it was not difficult to overlook such failures, the assumption being that software development was a cottage-industry craft and an art form and that following an engineering process somehow stifles creativity. In general, the marketplace was forgiving, driven primarily by its intense demand for software that would, it was hoped, provide solutions to its unique and often challenging problems. The product's developers failed to realize that their product sold because their product was either the only one available or that the alternatives that did exist were just simply worse than theirs.

However, such rationalizations no longer hold water. The software industry has matured into a solid engineering discipline while software applications have grown in size, complexity, and criticality. In addition, the marketplace possesses a more realistic understanding of what software products (and the industry at large) can deliver, and has become less tolerant of poor-quality products and draining, hidden maintenance costs.

To address many of the problems associated with the current state of the software development process, the International Standards Organization now provides the ISO 9000-3 guideline, henceforth referred to as the guideline, which, in effect, is a requirement being placed by customers upon many software development organizations. ISO 9000-3 does not tell software suppliers how to analyze, design, code, test, or document software products, but, instead, states that the supplier must have a process that is defined, clearly documented, and followed. ISO 9000-3 is based on the presupposition that, by following a defined engineering process, higher-quality software can be consistently brought to customers in a more timely manner.

Engineering a Software Product

To better understand how ISO 9000-3 attempts to improve upon the current state of software development, it is helpful to view how the software development process might function in an ideal world. The ideal can be compared to the more chaotic reality and from this comparison we can see how the ISO 9000-3 guideline can help.

In a calm and predictable world, we could decompose the entire software development process and view it from above in the following way:

The first step in the process creates a "shared map" of a customer's needs. The customer, representing diverse needs of various classes of user, and a systems engineer or marketing analyst begin a dialogue that results in a separation of the customer's actual needs from the customer's perceived needs and wants. A document is then created that represents these needs as rather high-level functional and technical requirements. These requirements are refined and prioritized by both the customer and the marketing analyst into a marketing requirements document.

With a common understanding and a prioritized list of the customer's needs, the software engineering organization can estimate preliminary costs of the efforts associated with developing a product. These estimates are based on the previously stated high-level requirements, the engineering organization's prior experience developing similar products, as well as a coherent, defined, and understood engineering process.

The customer's priorities and the estimated costs provide the quantifiable data and framework for making reasoned business decisions by organizational business management in order to create a working model of the product content, target costs, and delivery date.

Given an executive level go-ahead and a high-level product definition, the engineering organization begins a detailed analysis of the product requirements, producing preliminary yet detailed costs and schedules. Again, the cost estimates and preliminary schedules are based on quantifiable numbers derived from previous and similar efforts, a defined engineering process, and a chart of the customer's actual and prioritized needs.

The executive management reviews the estimated costs and schedules. If the numbers that engineering presents are reasonable, then the development process moves forward. If the numbers are not consistent with the original business goals for profitability and target product delivery dates, then one or several of the following business and engineering decisions must be made along with consideration of their consequences:

> The engineering process is tailored to reduce the cost and increase the risk to product reliability and maintainability.

> Requirements are modified or eliminated, which may cause a negative impact to sales and marketing effort.

> Head counts are increased to ship the product early, but smaller profit margins, due to increased costs, are accepted.

> Schedule and time to market are extended, but lower profits, due to entering the market late, are then risked.

It is important (imperative) that a balance is achieved between the marketing, business, and engineering organization's often conflicting roles and responsibilities. This balance often results in some undesirable risks that then must be managed as the development process continues. Once the budget, schedule, and technical goals and constraints have been identified, the engineering organization can begin its development process—designing, coding, documenting, and testing the software product. Engineering managers submit periodic status reports with quantifiable data to the business management. This type of information enables the management to recalibrate the development process, product definition, or business goals if the plans and actual development diverge (see Figure 2.1).

In the real product development world, however, the customer's needs generally are not identified in sufficient detail or clarity. Marketing or system engineering tries to rush through the analysis stages in order to shorten the time to market or to meet the customer's vaguely thought-out need date. Given a loosely stated set of vague and nonprioritized requirements, engineering goes through several iterations trying to determine what the product is supposed to be and the resources and schedule required to develop and deliver the product. To compound the problem, most engineering organizations typically do not have well-defined processes and, therefore, have no way of accurately estimating development costs and schedules.

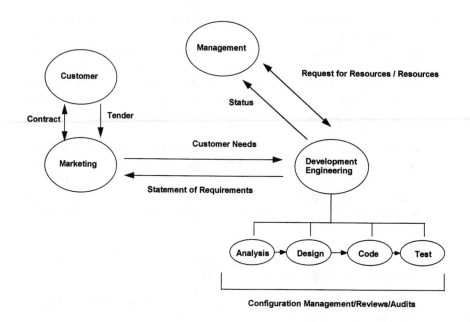

FIGURE 2.1. The business of software development.

Lacking accurate, clear, and prioritized requirements as well as cost estimates based on a discernible engineering process or prior efforts, the customer and the software supplier's marketing, engineering, and business management typically begin an extended discussion to determine the product's functionality, cost, schedule, and quality. Unfortunately, often this continues until a compromise, which pleases no one and rarely reflects the real requirements, cost, and schedule, is reached.

Once product development begins, there is little in the way of quantifiable or timely status reports. Lacking such information, management at all levels fails to make the changes in budget, schedule, process, or functionality that will most likely allow the organization's goals to match its capability to meet those goals within the current and foreseeable project environment. Risks that could have been identified at the beginning and all through the development effort are frequently left unidentified or unaddressed. As a consequence, managers at all levels are often surprised by the very risks they are supposed to manage.

The ISO 9000-3 Guideline

ISO 9000-3 provides a model for bringing the real and ideal worlds closer together. The guideline lays out the roles and responsibilities for both the customer and the supplier. It describes an engineering process that can be tailored, customized, and implemented any number of different ways. It also helps to create a common language for the customer, the software supplier, and all of the related organizations.

The guideline should be considered a customer requirement equal to or greater than any combination of functional or technical requirements. Those organizations that cannot show the use of a defined engineering process in the development of their software products may in the future find the market for their products and services more and more limited, not to mention being tied to expensive and exhaustive efforts to maintain the products they have already shipped.

The Software Engineering Process

Before we turn our attention to an analysis of the guideline, we believe it advisable to briefly summarize and define the highlights of the software engineering discipline. Note that there are a number of good books already written on the subject of software engineering. Our intention is not to repeat the information that you can readily find elsewhere. Instead, we will discuss software engineering at a high level to create a basis from which we can address and apply the guideline effectively.

If your organization is about to become (or is thinking about becoming) ISO certified, or if you intend to use the guideline in organizing engineering processes, then engineers and non-engineers alike will benefit from a common understanding as to what constitutes software engineering, that is, where it begins, where it ends, who is involved, and how it operates in its own development and business environment.

The following summary can serve as a starting point for the types of discussions that lead to an organization-wide agreement about the nature of the software engineering process in your company. This type of understanding is the first step toward creating an ISO 9000-3–compliant environment.

What Is Software Engineering?

There are a number of definitions of software engineering. A simple, straightforward one is as follows:

> Software engineering is a defined, step-by-step process that facilitates the specification, design, implementation, and testing of a software solution for a set of stated requirements in the most expeditious and cost-effective manner possible.

Software development and maintenance efforts should be based upon a defined process that

> serves as a basis for planning,

> provides a road map for implementing a software solution for a set of stated requirements,

has a process to control changes to the plans or road map, and

creates *succinct and usable* level of documentation that will support and facilitate continued enhancements to and maintenance of the product as well as provide the basis for estimating future efforts.

Also, engineering and management review processes should be defined to ensure the correctness of the work being performed as well as the appropriateness of the resources dedicated to the effort.

Decomposing Systems and Processes

Decomposition is a key concept that applies throughout the software engineering discipline. Decomposition is, essentially, the breaking down of large issues or problems into smaller, more manageable components that can be addressed or solved individually. A software product can be divided using functional decomposition or object-oriented methodologies into components that can be separately designed, coded, tested, and then reintegrated into a complete product.

Decomposition applies to the software development process as well. Here, a process can be decomposed into steps or subprocesses, each of which has specific inputs, outputs, and methodologies or mechanisms.

The software development process is composed of different phases that include analysis, design, code, test, integration (with other systems in the environment), and maintenance, and within each phase there may be a number of steps. Clearly defined phases and steps let us validate the input and the output of each phase or step. This gives us a way to identify and fix problems early on and learn how and why they arose in the first place. This way we can determine whether the problem was induced through a faulty process or a lack of processes, caused by a lack of knowledge or training, environmentally related, or created by a lack of proper management. Once the problems and their sources have been identified, solutions can be evaluated against cost estimates and available resources. Then, resources can be applied to fix each problem and eliminate its cause.

A Case for Plans, Specifications, Process, and Procedures

Before embarking on any effort in which you (an engineer or engineering manager) will be committing years of your life (and your mental and physical health), you may want to make sure that the goals of the effort have been identified. In addition, you should be sure that plans to reach those goals have been thought through, that procedures to implement the plans are in place, and that an environment has been created that is conducive to reaching the goals in the most expeditious manner possible.

In all engineering efforts there are specifications that describe what is to be built, how it will be built, and how it will be tested. Software development should be no different. Each step of the software development process should have:

customer or marketing requirements,

a specification that states what needs to be built,

methodologies and procedures that identify the way to fulfill the requirements for each step,

tests performed on the products or results of each step, and

quality goals to determine the risks involved with moving on to the next step in the development process.

No single software development process will work all the time and in every situation; however, there are fundamental principles, practices, and procedures on which all software development processes are based. The engineering process must be customized depending on schedules, budgets, quality goals, and the strengths and weaknesses inherent in a given organization.

ISO 9000-3 certification does not guarantee that an organization will create a high-quality product within a given set of technical, schedule, cost, and quality goals and constraints. However, by using the processes required to meet the ISO 9000-3 guideline, the chances are greatly increased.

The following pages provide a macroscopic view of the six phases that compose the software engineering process. In addition, you will find a description of configuration management that consists of the processes, mechanisms, and tools used by a given organization to gather, organize, and distribute the information and development products associated with the software life cycle. This high-level overview can serve as the basis for defining your organization's software or product development process. Again, every organization has different needs, uses different terminology and language, and produces products for different domains of activity. The specifics of your organization's process and how it is customized and tailored to meet its unique needs is not at issue here. What is important is that the people in your organization develop a common understanding of the software development process and each of its phases.

Phase 1: System Engineering/System Analysis

The goal of this phase is to identify and document the customer's needs and to build an understanding between the customer and the supplier as to the nature of the product that is to be developed. The input to phase 1 is a statement from the customer that identifies what it wants. The engineering process that operates during this phase is intended to extract, refine, and document the customer's needs, technical constraints, and product configurations. The output of phase 1 is usually called a System Specification, marketing requirements document, or a functional specification. This specification must be reviewed and agreed upon by both the customer and the supplier. The resulting document can act as the basis for a contract between the two organizations. This document must clearly specify a high-level set of requirements and articulate the essence of what the product is. By the end of phase 1, the customer and the supplier must have agreed upon the basic function and content of the product to be developed as well as the high-level statement of costs and schedules. This phase is performed by users, customers, marketing analysis, systems engineers, and, to a lesser extent, those who will be responsible for the development and testing of the product.

Phase 2: Software Requirements Analysis

The goal of this phase is to refine the high-level product requirements from phase 1 into detailed product requirements, which can be satisfied by a software product. The output of this step is a software requirements document that states in detail the specific functional requirements, external data flows, algorithms, error handling, and technical constraints. At the end of phase 2, the organization will have a detailed set of requirements that can be implemented and tested. In addition, the organization will have detailed costs and schedules for the various steps involved in implementation, testing, and documentation. Generally, this work is performed by software engineers, systems engineers, and test engineers.

Phase 3: Design

The goal of this phase is to create a design for the architectural, logical, error handling, user interface, data models, user documentation (including on-line help), and test cases needed to implement, describe, and test the requirements found in the software requirements specification. The output of this phase includes specifications that define the design, test cases, and user documentation. At the end of phase 3, the organization will have defined the structure (the underlying system of interdependencies of the product), which can then be implemented and tested. This phase is generally performed by software engineers, test engineers, and technical writers.

Phase 4: Implementation

The goals of this phase are to implement the design of the product as specified in the software design document, create the test cases to test the product, and produce a first version of the user documentation and/or on-line help. This phase includes code reviews, product testing at the component level, and review of the documentation. The outputs of phase 4 are components ready for higher levels of functional and system testing. A baseline is a work product that is closely related to other work products. Typically, changes to a baseline are likely to affect one or more other baselines and the efforts of more than one engineering group.

Examples of baselines include:

sanctioned technical documents such as product or project specifications, technical documentation, test plans, standards, and procedures;

source code;

development tools; and

test harnesses, test cases, test results, and test tools.

In addition, phase 4 provides the opportunity to continuously identify, log, and fix design defects. This phase is performed by software engineers, test engineers, and technical writers.

Phase 5: Testing

The goal of this phase is to test the product to ensure that it meets the requirements that were identified in the requirements specification. Testing follows a defined engineering process where requirements are traced to test cases, tests are run in a controlled environment, and updates to the product baseline are retested to ensure their correctness. The output of phase 5 is a software product that is ready to be shipped to the customer. In addition, test results and reports describing the testing that occurs are maintained. Design and implementation errors are identified, logged, and repaired on a case-by-case basis. Generally, this phase is performed by test engineers, as well as by the software engineers themselves.

Phase 6: Maintenance

The maintenance phase combines all the previous phases in a process used to enhance the product or fix problems that are identified once the product has been delivered. Unfortunately many engineers take a condescending attitude toward maintenance; they and many non-software managers fail to understand the difficulty involved with making changes to a product without introducing bugs. Maintenance, generally speaking, requires more skill and better management than was required in the original development.

Configuration Control

To facilitate the software development process so that the product meets its functional and quality requirements and goals, software engineering control processes are necessary. Organizations must formalize and install some type of configuration control system to manage code, documentation, and project baselines. In addition, it is important to have a formal work product review process during all six product development phases to ensure the quality of the incremental work products that compose the final product.

Configuration control is the central control mechanism for the software engineering process. It includes tools, processes, and procedures to provide the way to identify, control access to, and manage changes to both product and project baselines.

The first objective of configuration control is to establish project and product baselines. In addition to identifying these baselines, configuration control must provide a means to control the processing of both internal and external change requests that affect those baselines. A change request is a formal way of requesting a change to an established baseline.

The intention of controlling the baselines through processes and procedures is to document and expedite necessary changes to baselines while concurrently preventing unnecessary, untimely, and unauthorized changes. By reviewing and analyzing proposed changes, the ripple effect of requested changes throughout other baselines and the product can be identified, costed, and scheduled. Configuration control also ensures that the requested changes are actually made to the product baselines once they have been committed.

Typically, a configuration control board (CCB) manages the change process by reviewing, authorizing, and approving changes to product baselines. The membership of the CCB may consist of the program manager, marketing manager, engineering project manager, technical documentation manager, and a test or quality manager. The CCB meets on a periodic basis; minutes are taken, new action items are assigned, and previous action items are reviewed.

Reviews, Inspections, and Walk-Throughs

Covering the entire software development process is an umbrella activity of technical reviews. Some reviews are meant to allow the purchaser and supplier to come to agreement on such issues as product features, schedule, cost, and responsibilities. Other reviews allow engineers to find, correct, and minimize the impacts of errors. For instance, an error caught during a design review is less expensive than the same error caught during testing or after a customer has taken possession of the product. From an engineering management perspective reviews help find and eliminate the cause of the errors, confirm the development process, build teamwork, and improve engineers' capability.

Those responsible for the management, specification, development, testing, and continued support of a product should know what type of review should be done, when, by whom, and what the goal of the various types of reviews are. Management must show commitment to the review process by allocating resources and reviewing the written reports produced by the process.

Product Quality

Software quality is a somewhat elusive goal. Most people base their estimate of a product's quality on its functionality and the appearance of the user interface. There are other attributes of a product besides functionality that, taken as a whole, determine the quality of a product. The software industry refers to these as the "-ilities" as in reliability, testability, portability, usability, extensibility, and maintainability.

Reliability is the degree to which the product meets its functionality over a measured period of time. Testability is the measure of difficulty in testing a product. For instance, a product that takes four weeks to test has less quality, in this regard, than a product that takes four days to test. Portability is the measure of effort required to modify and test a product to allow that product to run in an environment other than that for which it was developed. Usability is the measure of ease in learning and using the product. Extensibility refers to the ease of enhancing the product, and maintainability is more narrowly focused on making updates to deal with bugs in the system. All of the "-ilities" are rarely considered by the supplier or by the purchaser and yet, along with functionality they are the attributes that determine whether one is dealing with a "quality" product.

3

ISO 9000-3: Theory, Concept, Themes, Interpretation, and Critique

To provide a deeper understanding of the guideline, we discuss the theories, concepts, and themes that form the guideline's philosophical basis. We also present several criticisms of an otherwise excellent document, especially focusing on the sometimes inexact and widespread use of the term "quality." Also, for the reader to have a better understanding of our interpretation of the guideline, we briefly discuss the manner in which we deal with the documentation required for the Quality Policy, Quality Manual, and Quality Plan that make up so much of the ISO 9000 literature.

Theory

The theory behind the ISO 9000-3 is that a well-managed organization with a defined engineering process is more likely to produce products that *consistently* meet the purchaser's requirements, within schedule and budget, than a poorly managed organization that lacks an engineering process. Consequently, purchasers of software goods and services would be wise if they purchase software goods and services only from those suppliers who possess a demonstrated engineering and engineering management capability.

Concept

The major concept in the ISO 9000-3 guideline is that software development and maintenance is a varied but integrated engineering process made up of distinct phases, steps, procedures, and activities. This process requires an equally integrated management approach based on senior management's stating a policy that requires the use of engineering practices in the development of a product, and on the subordinate levels of management's developing plans to implement that policy and managing their individual plans. All levels of management stay involved with the development effort through reviews and audits of the various projects. Based on these reviews, management tailors the development process to optimize the balance between schedule, cost, functionality, reliability, and usability.

Themes

There are three major themes that make up the ISO 9000-3 guideline. First, both purchaser and supplier management have responsibilities. Supplier management is responsible for the creation of an engineering organization and the institution and use of an engineering process. Supplier management must specify a high-level policy guideline that is meant to ensure the organization's focus on development of a quality product. The guideline refers to this document as the Quality Policy.

Purchaser management is responsible for ensuring that the requirements for the product or service are explicitly stated, that requests for changes to those requirements are authorized, and that the purchaser organization is prepared to assume ownership of the product after performing acceptance testing.

The second theme is that an engineering process is made up of several phases, with defined inputs and outputs to those phases. These phases are purchaser requirement analysis, design, implementation, test, and maintenance. There are defined roles and responsibilities for the various engineers who implement that process, and means to test the products and by-products of that engineering process. The requirement for this process springs from the Quality Policy, and the process makes up the Quality System as described in section 4.2.1 of the guideline. In addition, the engineering process must be managed by plans that identify schedule, resources, and statusing mechanisms, and review and audit procedures required to develop the product and ensure that the product meets the purchaser's requirements.

The third theme is that there are activities that support engineering development, test, and documentation processes. These activities are configuration management (the control of product project baselines), document control, product and process quality measurement, and training. Plans for the implementation of these activities need to be developed and resources committed to carry out the plans.

Interpretation

The guideline calls for a documented engineering process, supported by reviews of the process's products and audits of the process itself. In addition, plans for resources to implement the process, reviews, and audits must be in place and the resources adequate to meet the plan's requirements.

The first document the company needs is the Quality Policy. The Quality Policy is authored by the highest level of company management. The Quality Policy at a minimum is a short, direct statement meant to apply to all departments within a company. Basically it is meant to identify the company's senior management's commitment to quality and the approach to be adopted in pursuit of quality objectives. We believe that the approach should be a broad statement requiring the various organizations that make up the company (i.e., engineering, marketing, sales, and finance) to follow commonly accepted engineering and business practices in the performance of their duties. In addition, the senior management should use Quality Policy to outline the roles, responsibilities, and expectations for those organizations.

The above interpretation is somewhat unorthodox, but keep in mind that one of the basic themes in the ISO program is that senior management must be involved in creating an engineering environment. Unless that level of management gives broad yet clear direction as to what constitutes an engineering environment, a company will spend hundreds if not thousands of hours debating the need for such an environment and the direction the company should take in creating that environment. To put it more plainly, the goal of senior management is to maximize profit. To do so, a company must utilize its resources in the most effective manner possible. Therefore, management's primary responsibility must be to ensure that the most efficient engineering and business practices and procedures are in use within the company and that the organizations that make up the company are united in their understanding concerning their roles, responsibilities, and expectations. Without this common understanding it is doubtful whether a company can create reliable products in a consistent manner. For this reason the Quality Policy must be something more than just a general statement concerning a company's commitment to quality. We suggest that the Quality Policy be a statement from the most senior manager in the organization. This statement should describe at a high level the roles, responsibilities, and expectations for the various organizations that report to this manager. In addition, the Quality Policy should direct that all work should be performed according to sound engineering and business practices except where otherwise authorized. From this policy can evolve the quality (i.e., engineering and business) practices required to create reliable products in a consistent manner.

The guideline identifies the Quality Process as the implementation of the Quality Policy. The Quality Process must be documented. Much of the literature associated with the ISO 9000 movement refers to this document as the Quality Manual. Again, we feel that lumping everything under the term "quality" serves only to confuse and cloud the issues associated with engineering a product; therefore, we refer to the document used to define the process for developing software as the software process handbook (SPH). The SPH defines the engineering process that implements the Quality Policy. The SPH must be reviewed and approved by the company's senior management to ensure that it meets the goals of the Quality Policy.

The guideline, as written, has a great deal of overlap and repetition between the software process handbook (our term for the Quality Manual), the quality plan, and the development plan. This overlap can be quite confusing. We assume that each development and maintenance project has a plan that identifies the resources, schedules, and specific approach required to implement the engineering process identified in the software process handbook, especially the analysis, design, and coding phases. We refer to this plan as the software development plan. We also assume this plan will include or reference subordinate plans (i.e., configuration management plan, test plan, document control plan).

We feel there is a definite need for a quality assurance plan, but the plan should focus on identifying the activities, schedules, and resources required to perform audits of the process, verification of external deliverables, failure analysis, and metrics gathering and reporting. Consequently, we identify only these topics as being in the quality assurance plan.

Critique

One general criticism of the guideline is over the use of the term "quality." The guideline correctly states that any practice, procedure, activity, or person involved at any level in the specification, development, test, and maintenance of the software product is engaged in an activity that impacts quality. By lumping everything under the heading "quality," the guideline blurs the lines between the engineering activities used to develop and maintain the product (e.g., analysis, design, code, test, configuration control, reviews), and those engineering activities that fall under the heading of Quality Assurance (e.g., audits, inspections, metrics), which are used to assure the quality of the product and the development process. In addition, by making everyone responsible for "quality" the guideline makes it difficult for an organization to clearly define roles, responsibilities, and authority of the individuals engaged in engineering activities and quality assurance activities.

A second criticism is that the guideline seems to have skipped over one of the commonly accepted phases in software engineering, the detailed software requirements phase. On any project of reasonable size and complexity there is a detailed requirements analysis phase used to turn high-level purchaser requirements into detailed requirements that can be implemented and tested. The guideline moves from identifying the purchaser's requirements (section 5.3), to discussing development planning, and then picks up the engineering process at design before moving into implementation.

A third criticism is the guideline requirement for a quality plan (section 5.5). As stated in the guideline, the quality plan identifies a number of topics, many of which belong in the documents that define the engineering process or the specific plans for developing and testing a product. For instance, "defined input and output for each development phase and the types of tests and verification and validation activities to be carried out" should be defined as part of the engineering process. In addition, the "detailed planning of test, verification, and validation including schedules, resources, and approval authorities" belong in the software development plan (section 5.4.2) or the test plan (section 5.7.2). Furthermore the specific re-sponsibilities for the implementation of "configuration management, change con-trol, defect control, and corrective action" is specifically addressed in the configu-ration management plan (sections 6.1.2 through 6.1.3.2).

We believe that many of the quality activities identified in the guideline's quality plan are really commonly accepted engineering activities and should be fully inte-grated in the definition of the engineering process and the plans to implement that process. On the other hand, activities such as quality assurance audits, inspections, and metrics belong in a quality plan in that they are not involved in developing software but rather in assuring and measuring the product's quality.

The fourth criticism concerns section 5.4.2 of the guideline, which addresses the contents of the development plan. We feel that section 5.4.2.1 can be somewhat misleading. For instance, the guideline says, "The development plan should define a disciplined process or methodology for transforming the purchaser's requirements specification into a software product." Our criticism hinges on the word "define." The "disciplined process" should already have been defined when the organization documented its Quality Process; there is no need to redefine it in the development plans required for each development effort. A plan is meant to identify a specific implementation of an engineering process and the resources and schedules required to implement that process.

The fifth criticism is a minor one. Section 5.4.2.1 of the guideline seems to overlap succeeding sections. "Identification" of inputs, outputs, and verification procedures for each development phase is addressed in Input to Development Phases (section 5.4.4), Output from Development Phases (section 5.4.5), and Ver-ification of Each Phase (section 5.4.6). Basically, section 5.4.2.1 should be deleted or have its title changed to "General." This section should be rewritten to state that the sections following 5.4.2.1 are meant to identify the specific implementation of the defined engineering process and the resources required to implement that process.

Criticism and Warning

The sixth criticism is both a criticism and serious warning to organizations that plan to use this guideline to structure their engineering organization. Section 4.1.1.2.3, Management Representative, states that a management representative "shall have defined authority and responsibility for ensuring that the requirements of [ISO 9001] are implemented." The key word here is "ensuring." When an individual has been given the responsibility and authority to "ensure" something happens, then that person can give management and technical direction to other managers or individuals. This person now has "line" as opposed to "staff" authority. Assigning this responsibility and authority to a "staff" manager will almost certainly cause friction with "line" managers.

Organizations should decide where budget and schedule responsibilities lie and assign the manager with those responsibilities the "authority and responsibility for ensuring that the requirements of [ISO 9001] are implemented," or be prepared to spend many hours in heated debate over who has what authority and responsibility for giving technical or managerial direction that can affect budgets and schedules.

We suggest that a senior line manager be made responsible for ensuring the requirements are implemented. This senior manager could assign other managers or engineers to audit the process and report to the manager the results of their audit. Based on the reports, this senior manager could give the direction required to ensure the requirements are implemented while at the same time assume the responsibility for any impact to schedule, budget, and quality. A second suggestion is to have a senior manager, possibly at the director level, whose responsibility would be to install a quality assurance program that reviews engineering efforts, gathers metrics, provides training, and reports to the organization's senior executive. Technical direction remains the province of the line managers, and the quality assurance group can maintain its objectivity when reviewing the work of others and still have direct input to the organization's development process through the offices of the senior executive.

4

ISO 9000-3:
Scope and Overview

Many readers and users of the guideline will skip over this chapter or give it only superficial attention. This would be a mistake. This chapter discusses the guideline's scope and provides an overview of the guideline. We strongly recommend that the reader go through this chapter several times in order to gain a high-level understanding of the guideline. Without this level of understanding the reader may become lost in the details of following chapters or confused by the repetitiveness sometimes exhibited by the guideline. Failure to "see the forest for the trees" will affect the reader's understanding of how the management and engineering processes described in each section are meant to support the development and maintenance of a quality product.

There are two key concepts discussed in this chapter. The first concept is that the guideline is identifying "guidelines." The guideline does not dictate the use of any procedure or process. The guideline identifies what are commonly accepted, sound engineering and engineering management practices that are "suggested" for use in development or maintenance of a product. An engineering organization needs to establish its own engineering and management practices and procedures, and the guideline provides excellent guidelines and suggestions in those areas. It is important to understand and not make assumptions that you need a very complicated, super-detailed implementation to be ISO compliant. Instead, focus on the essential requirements and tailor your process to the size of your organization and the criticality of the application.

The second concept (more ours than the guideline's) is that use of the guideline need not be limited to instances where there is a second-party purchaser of a supplier's software but can also be used for in-house development efforts. This type of relationship exists to some degree in almost all situations where software is being developed or maintained. The guideline can be a powerful tool for any software organization to improve its products and services. For example, information systems or automation systems developed by in-house engineers (suppliers) are used by in-house customers (purchasers) in order to meet organizational goals. Organizations that develop software for sale to specific industries or the general public have a purchaser/supplier relationship between marketing (purchaser) and engineering (supplier). And possibly more important than the previous two examples is where embedded software is used to control a product whose failure could cause significant financial loss or physical harm. All of the guidelines apply to these situations and should be used whenever possible and feasible.

In this and following chapters we have used boldface type for the section numbers and words that are taken directly from the guideline. In the overview portion of this chapter we discuss the key sections while passing over several sections that are merely high-level numbers or contain only general remarks.

1   Scope

Comment: In this and subsequent chapters we follow the numbering system as given by the guideline. Throughout, we use boldface to signify extracts from the guideline. Following the extract are our comments and recommendations.

This part of ISO 9000 sets out guidelines to facilitate the application of ISO 9001 to organizations developing, supplying and maintaining software.

Comment: The key word here is "facilitate." The guideline presents engineering guidelines, whose use is not meant to slow the development process but rather to eliminate the confusion and errors that are the root cause of late, over-budget, and poor-quality products.

It is intended to provide guidance where a contract between two parties requires the demonstration of a supplier's capability to develop, supply and maintain software products.

Comment: This is a key statement. Many engineers recognize the need for better engineering and management processes and procedures, but their management fails to see a need for such processes and procedures. The guideline (and the certification process) is now a market-driven need in the sense that potential purchasers of the supplier's products will require (through the certification process) the implementation of recognized engineering and management processes and procedures. Again, we emphasize that the guideline should also be used for products developed within an organization that are meant to be used "in-house" by other members of the organization.

The guidelines in this part of ISO 9000 are applicable in contractual situations for software products when

a) the contract specifically requires design effort and the product require-

ments are stated principally in performance terms, or they need to be established;

Comment: The guideline is pointing out the importance of identifying the products requirements in a quantifiable manner so that it can be determined through some form of testing (i.e., demonstration, analysis, or inspection) that the product meets purchaser requirements.

b) confidence in the product can be attained by the adequate demonstration of a certain supplier's capabilities in development, supply and maintenance.

Comment: The guideline is requiring proof that a supplier can actually perform the development and maintenance activities required *before* the supplier is put on contract.

2 Normative References

This section identifies the provisions that are referenced in the text and are part of the ISO 9000. The references are as follows:

ISO 2382-1:1984, *Data processing—Vocabulary—Part 01: Fundamental terms*

ISO 8402:1986, *Quality—Vocabulary.*

ISO 9001:1987, *Quality systems—Model for quality assurance in design/development, production, installation and servicing*

3 Definitions

This section defines several terms used in the guideline.

3.1 **software: Intellectual creation comprising the programs, procedures, rules and any associated documentation pertaining to the operation of a data processing system.**

3.2 **software product: Complete set of computer programs, procedures and associated documentation and data designated for delivery to a user.**

3.3 **software item: Any identifiable part of a software product at an intermediate step or at the final step of development.**

3.4 **development: All activities to be carried out to create a software product.**

3.5 **phase: Defined segment of work.**

3.6 verification (for software): The process of evaluating the products of a given phase to ensure correctness and consistency with respect to the products and standards provided as input to that phase.

3.7 validation (for software): The process of evaluating software to ensure compliance with specified requirements.

4   Quality System—Framework

4.1   Management Responsibility

This is an exceptionally important point in that senior management must be seen as being active in the definition and implementation of an engineering process within their organization. The purpose of this section is to ensure that both senior supplier and purchaser management are aware of their responsibilities. It is management's responsibility to ensure that individuals within the organization know and understand their role and responsibilities. It is also management's responsibility to ensure that supplier and purchaser organizations are communicating effectively.

The supplier management must

create an engineering environment with clearly identified roles and responsibilities for the engineers who work in the environment,

identify and provide the resources needed to verify the engineering work being performed is accurate and complete,

ensure that defined practices and procedures are being followed, and

take part themselves in the review of the engineering and engineering practices and procedures to ensure their suitability and effectiveness.

The purchaser management should

ensure the supplier has all the purchaser-specific information needed to meet contractual obligations, and

identify one purchaser representative responsible for supplier interface.

Both purchaser management and supplier management should ensure that joint reviews take place on a regular basis. The purpose of these reviews is to verify completeness and accuracy of requirements, supplier verification test results, and purchaser acceptance test results.

4.2   Quality System

Management must first identify its organization's goals and then ensure the existence of an engineering environment where those goals can be reached in the most efficient manner possible. This section identifies management's responsibility to ensure the existence of an engineering environment that has

> defined processes and procedures;

> development and maintenance plans based on the defined process and procedures;

> reviews, audits, and tests to determine the quality of the product(s) being created and the process used to create those products; and

> corrective actions based on the information gained from reviews, audits, and tests.

4.3   Internal Quality System Audits

This section identifies the requirement for an internal audit process to ensure that the engineering process used by the company is in fact meeting the company's product and process quality goals. Documented findings from the audits are to be reviewed and acted upon by those responsible for the areas or processes audited.

4.4   Corrective Action

This section identifies a requirement for a "closed loop" management process to ensure that the causes of quality problems are determined and that actions are taken to control the problems with the product and address the changes in practices and procedures required to avoid recurrence of the problem.

5   Quality System—Life-Cycle Activities

5.1   General

Section 5.1 is really a disclaimer. The guideline states that all development projects (and maintenance projects) should follow an organized life cycle (or process). The disclaimer is that nothing in the guideline requires or implies that any specific life cycle be followed. Suppliers are free to use any life cycle they deem best suited for the type of product being developed, or maintained, as long as consideration is given to the various activities referred to in Sections 5.2 through 5.10 as life-cycle activities. These activities are the basic activities found in a managed software process.

5.2 Contract Review

This section identifies the need for the purchaser and supplier to come to an agreement on contractual obligations and the need to identify methods for resolving contract issues that may arise between the purchaser and supplier. Both purchaser and supplier management need to understand

> the scope of the contract,

> its organization's responsibilities,

> risks (e.g., schedule, budget, legal) to its organizations, and

> ownership of the product and by-products.

5.3 Purchaser's Requirements Specification

This section focuses on the need to identify the product's functional and technical (e.g., performance, safety, reliability, etc.) requirements as well as the product's external interface. The purchaser and supplier have a responsibility to work together to ensure these requirements are complete and quantifiable before product development begins.

5.4 Development Planning

5.4.1 General

This short section identifies several basic principles of software project management.

5.4.2 Development Plan

Once a purchaser's requirements have been identified there needs to be a development plan to deliver a product that meets those requirements. The development plan identifies the resources and schedule required to deliver a product. The resources and schedule are based upon a combination of the purchaser's requirements, engineering practices, and procedures used by the supplier to meet those requirements and the purchaser's need date for the product.

This section identifies the need for a development plan to show

> the phases of development,

> inputs and outputs to each phase,

> schedule and resources for each phase,

> progress status and control,

> tools and methods to be used, and

> verification procedures for each phase (reviews, audits, and testing).

5.4.3   Progress Control

This section briefly discusses the need to ensure the proper researching of a project throughout the entire life cycle.

5.4.4   Input to Development Phases

This section points out that each development phase should have defined inputs and that each product requirement should be stated in such a manner as to be quantifiably tested.

5.4.5   Output from Development Phases

The outputs of one step in the software development process are the inputs into the next step. These outputs should be validated to ensure that they meet the requirements of the next step and have been engineered in such a manner as to be a quality product.

5.4.6   Verification of Each Phase

This section states that the output of each phase should be tested in some manner to ensure its fitness for use in the next phase.

5.5   Quality Planning

There are activities used to verify or validate the quality of a development effort's products or by-products. This section suggests that plans be defined to ensure that these activities take place. The plans for these activities can be a separate plan (a software quality assurance plan) or incorporated in other plans like the development plan, test plan, and configuration management plan.

To a large degree this section is redundant in that it repeats, or overlaps with, subjects found in other sections of the guideline in its discussion of

defining inputs and outputs for each development phase;

identifying the types of test to be carried out;

identifying the resources, schedules, and roles and responsibilities for carrying out the tests;

configuration management; and

defect control and corrective action.

As mentioned in an earlier criticism, having a separate plan to identify the resources and schedules needed to implement the quality activities identified in this section is contrary to the goal of having these activities integrated into the other engineering process and procedures used to create a quality product.

5.6   Design and Implementation

5.6.1   General

This section is a general statement that points out that design and implementation are the processes that turn purchaser requirements into a product.

5.6.2   Design

Design is the technical kernel of a software product and to a great degree dictates the quality of the product. How well a product is designed especially impacts the product's usability and the costs to maintain and enhance the product throughout its lifetime. The guideline suggests the design effort and the product itself would benefit from considering the following:

design methodologies,

design rules and guidelines,

internal design (not seen by the user), and

comparison to previous designs.

5.6.3   Implementation

The guideline is very light in its suggested guidelines in some sections and this section is one of them. The guideline suggests that the supplier establish and use guidelines for mundane subjects such as naming conventions, coding, and comments.

5.6.4   Reviews

The section addresses the need for the supplier to review the products of analysis, design, implementation, and testing in order to ensure that the final product meets the purchaser's requirements. Reviews and inspections are also meant to ensure that the methodologies and rules that were meant to be used during design were actually used. Therefore, the first goal is meant to validate a product and the second goal is meant to verify that the product was created using the organization's practices, procedures, and methodologies, the latter being a quality assurance function.

5.7   Testing and Validation

5.7.1   General

This section states that a multilevel testing process may be used to test a product and that a plan should be in place to support controlling the testing process.

5.7.2   Test Planning

There are various levels of testing that can be performed on a software product. There need to be plans in place to support this process. The plans should address

> types of testing,
>
> test cases,
>
> test environment,
>
> resources and schedule required to create the tests,
>
> resources and schedule required to execute the tests, and
>
> test completion criteria.

5.7.3   Testing

This section identifies general practices that should be followed in the testing software products. The guideline suggests that test results should be recorded and used in order to

> identify problems with the product being tested,
>
> identify areas where tests need to be rerun, and
>
> determine the adequacy of the test process.

5.7.4   Validation

The guideline considers validation as the testing that is performed by the supplier on a version of the product that is intended to be delivered to the purchaser. Software testing can occur before validation, but that type of testing is, according to the guideline, verification of a product's components as opposed to validation of an entire product.

5.7.5   Field Testing

Field testing takes place at a site other than the supplier's that is as close to an operational environment as possible. The guideline suggests that the field tests need to be planned and that the supplier and purchaser may need to coordinate their efforts in the support of this type of testing.

5.8   Acceptance (Testing)

Acceptance testing is performed by the purchaser. The guideline points out the need for this to be a formal process planned well in advance of the actual testing. An acceptance test plan should identify the schedule, resources, roles and responsibilities, success criteria, and problem handling procedures well before the actual tests are executed. The guideline also emphasizes that the supplier and purchaser have a shared responsibility for testing that goes on in this phase and must work closely together.

5.9   Replication, Delivery and Installation

Replication and delivery are straightforward processes that are performed after a product has been developed or enhanced and must now be sent to a purchaser. Installation, on the other hand, may require coordination between the purchaser and the supplier. The level of coordination depends upon the complexity of the product and the number of purchaser sites that use the product. Installation planning should address schedules, available personnel, site access, availability and access to systems and equipment, and testing.

5.10   Maintenance

The guideline points out that product maintenance, or enhancement, has the same components as product development. Analysis, design, implementation, and testing of changes to the product must all be planned, scheduled, and performed. The guideline points out that the purchaser and the supplier must agree as to the timing and content of products releases so that both the supplier and purchaser can support the rate of product release.

6   Quality System—Supporting Activities

6.1   Configuration Management

Configuration management is the process by which a product's baselines (e.g., requirements, source code, test cases, test results, user documentation, etc.) are identified and changes to those baselines are controlled. The guideline identifies the need for an engineering organization to identify, define, and plan for

identification of product baselines,

version control of the product baselines,

roles and responsibilities of the engineering organizations in the change process,

change control procedures, and

status of the change control processes and baseline products.

6.2   Document Control

Engineering is a specification-driven process. There are a number of different engineering documents used in the development and maintenance of a software product. The guideline identifies the need for an engineering organization to identify and control the use of these documents. Control is especially important for the initial approval and dissemination of such documents and the authorization and reissue of updated versions.

6.3   Quality Records

Engineering organizations should maintain records that document the quality of their processes and products. Records of reviews, audits, and test results should be maintained to allow for their use in process and organizational improvement. The guideline suggests that procedures and processes should be identified and implemented to control the accumulation, storage, and retrieval of such documents.

6.4   Measurement

Engineering management should be a closed-loop process where measurements are taken to determine the quality of the products and processes used to create or manage those products. The guideline states that product measurement is based on purchaser/customer feedback and internal audits performed by the supplier organization. These measurements are needed for product and process improvement. The guideline suggests that process measurement is used to determine whether schedule milestones are being met and whether the by-products of the process are meeting their quality goals. The guideline points out that for measurements to be useful an organization needs to identify the current level of performance, improvement goals, measurement data to be collected, and actions to be taken based on measuring data against goals.

6.5   Rules, Practices and Conventions

This section of the guideline suggests the need for the supplier organization to document the engineering practices and procedures that are used to develop and maintain software products and revise them as necessary.

6.6   Tools and Techniques

In this section the guideline suggests that the supplier should identify and use "tools, facilities, and techniques" in the development and management of software products and replace or improve the tools, facilities, and techniques as necessary.

6.7   Purchasing

In this and the following section the guideline points out that concerning third-party products, the supplier should apply many of the same management and engineering techniques as the purchaser uses in relation to the supplier. For example, the supplier (now acting as a purchaser) should ensure the subcontractor's ability to perform the contracted work and validate the subcontractor's products.

6.8   Included Software Product

A supplier may have third-party products that need to be integrated with its own products. The supplier should identify procedures to ensure these products meet stated quality goals and that procedures and plans are in place for the storage, protection, and maintenance of the third-party products.

6.9   Training

Engineers need to be trained in order to meet their responsibilities. An engineering organization must identify the techniques, tools, procedures, and methodologies that are used in the development and maintenance of a product. Once these have been identified, then a program can be instituted to ensure that engineers are proficient in their use.

5
Supplier Management Responsibility

Supplier management, at the organization level, has two basic responsibilities: (1) to ensure that the engineering environment is based on a defined engineering process, with engineers trained to work within that environment; (2) to ensure that the engineering process is being used and is effective in producing products that meet or exceed the product's requirements (i.e., functionality, reliability, maintainability, testability, usability, and supportability).

To meet these responsibilities, supplier management must

state its policy concerning the use of engineering practices and procedures,

emphasize that product nonconformance will be dealt with immediately and directly,

ensure that all engineers understand and adhere to this policy, and

identify the individuals and resources required to verify the use of the engineering practices and procedures used to develop products.

4 Quality System—Framework

4.1 Management Responsibility

4.1.1 Supplier's Management Responsibility

4.1.1.1 Quality Policy

The supplier's management shall define and document its policy and objectives

for, and commitment to, quality. The supplier shall ensure that this policy is understood, implemented and maintained at all levels in the organization.

Reason: In many organizations, senior management has little or no direct input into the manner in which software is developed. A defined, documented, company-wide policy on quality and quality objectives is the link from this level of management to the project-level management. Without this commitment from the highest level of management, the individual project's management, and the various organizations and engineers performing on those projects, may have differing views of quality and the process and procedures required to obtain it. Confusion, duplication of effort, and inconsistency in the work required to obtain quality in both process and product will most likely result.

Means to ensure: Senior management should work with the project-level management to define a high-level organization-wide quality policy. This policy should state that software development shall follow an engineering process and identify that process at a high level. Every member of the engineering organization should read this policy statement and be able to summarize its basic tenets.

4.1.1.2   Organization

4.1.1.2.1   Responsibility and Authority

The responsibility, authority and the interrelation of all personnel who manage, perform and verify work affecting quality shall be defined; particularly for personnel who need the organizational freedom and authority to . . .

Comment: This section and the following subsections speak to the need for defined engineering process and the roles of those individuals and organizations that are responsible for implementing the process. Currently, many organizations rely upon an informal process. This informal process may occasionally work for small groups of focused engineers but not in larger or more complex environments.

Reason: Virtually everyone's work affects the quality of the process or the product. Many companies fail to identify the "responsibility, authority, and relationship" between the different organizations of a company that have a role in the development of the product. This failure can lead to overlapping responsibility and authority with the consequences being confusion or gaps in the engineering process or management of that process.

Means to ensure: The Quality Policy should identify and define the responsibilities, authority, and relationships of the various organizations. Included in these responsibilities is the need for each organization to document the processes and procedures required to meet its responsibilities. The Quality Policy should require a review by senior management of the processes and procedures as defined by the various organizations.

a) initiate action to prevent the occurrence of product nonconformity;

Comment: This is a wide-open statement that can be interpreted broadly. The authors have chosen to focus on the word "initiate." We believe that anyone can initiate action to prevent the occurrence of product nonconformity. This initiation can range from writing a bug report to holding a walk-through to executing a test. It is the responsibility of management to determine whether, once initiated, the bug report or the results of the walk-through or tests require action to prevent nonconformity.

Reason: An engineering process has checks and balances in the form of reviews and tests. Senior management must ensure that a system of checks and balances is in place and that the system is being exercised.

Means to ensure: The Quality Policy should state that product development shall follow a defined and documented engineering process to include the need for quality related process (e.g., tests, reviews, configuration management). This engineering process, as documented in the software process handbook (SPH), identifies the practices and procedures that are followed by project-level managers and engineers in regard to initiating and implementing steps used to prevent nonconformance.

Some organizations' Quality Policy may even go so far as to identify a separate software process quality assurance (SPQA) organization with authority to engage in quality-related activities such as process audits, and give this organization the authority to initiate action to prevent nonoccurrence.

b) identify and record any product quality problems;

Reason: Identifying a problem is the first step to solving it. Recording the problem ensures that the problem will not be lost or misunderstood. Additionally, documenting product quality problems provides the basis for a quality metrics program.

Means to ensure: The Quality Policy should state that the various engineering organizations are responsible for creating, documenting, and implementing a formal process to identify and record quality problems. The SPH defines this process and has templates for the documentation used to support the process.

c) initiate, recommend or provide solutions through designated channels;

Reason: Many organizations rely upon informal procedures for dealing with nonconformance in the products they develop or maintain. Relying solely upon informal procedures may result in some problems receiving only partial solutions, the wrong organizations addressing the problem, or reinventing "new" solutions for an old problem.

Means to ensure: The SPH identifies the process used to provide a solution and identifies the organizations responsible for implementing the solution. This process is discussed in more detail in section 6.1, Configuration Management.

d) verify the implementation of solutions;

Reason: The problem-solving process is often an open-ended activity and in many instances lacks an explicit, objective check as to whether the solution has solved the problem. Once a solution to a problem has been applied, a determination must be made whether the solution solved the problem and has not introduced other problems.

Means to ensure: The Quality Policy should state that changes to the product are to be tested. The SPH identifies the practices, procedures, and groups responsible for validating the changes. In the case of the final software product, this is usually a separate test organization. For other components that make up the product (e.g., documentation, design documents, test cases), it is usually the responsibility of the managers responsible for those products. If the solution required necessitates changes to the engineering process as defined in the SPH, then the engineering manager responsible for the definition and implementation of the process must approve the change (see section 4.1.1.2.3).

e) control further processing, delivery or installation of nonconforming product until the deficiency or unsatisfactory condition has been corrected.

Reason: Note that the guideline says "control further processing" as opposed to prevent or prohibit further processing. There are times when a defect is acceptable, as long as its impact is known and there are "work-arounds" that allow a product to be continued to be developed or used. There are numerous instances where this is permissible. For instance, specifications, documents, and test cases may not be complete. In instances like these, TBDs (To Be Determined) may be identified and, once documented and agreed to, would allow further development. Other examples are when problems in the design of the product exist but development can continue with code and test cases created for those sections of the product that have passed a design review. Additionally, many products are shipped that have known defects with documented work-arounds that allow the purchaser to use the product with minimum risk.

Means to ensure: The Quality Policy should explicitly address the subject of continued development or product delivery when there are known problems in the product. The Quality Process should state that this is acceptable, but require management review and authorization. Management should require a plan to eliminate the nonconformance and show how the nonconformance will be controlled to allow continued development or use. Records of these reviews should be kept.

4.1.1.2.2   Verification Resources and Personnel

The supplier shall identify in-house verification requirements, provide adequate resources and assign trained personnel for verification activities.

Reason: It is commonly accepted that an engineering process includes verification steps. If senior management requires verification activities to be part of the development and maintenance of a product, then it must provide the resources to implement those activities.

Means to ensure: The Quality Policy should state that verification of the engineering process (and validation of the products) is part of the engineering process used in a product's development and maintenance. The SPH should identify the various verification activities and the organizations responsible for implementing those activities. The software development plan (SDP) should identify the resources and schedules required to train personnel to implement those activities and to carry them out.

Verification activities shall include inspection, test and monitoring of the design, production, installation and servicing process and/or product;

Reason: This statement identifies a general verification and validation process. Verification ensures that the engineering process is taking place through inspection, monitoring, or auditing. Validation ensures the correctness of the product through formal testing. Several sections in the guideline discuss the inspection, testing, and monitoring involved in an engineering process.

Means to ensure: Include this statement from the guideline or a similar one in the Quality Policy and have the SPH detail its implementation when describing reviews, audits, testing, and configuration management. The SDP identifies the schedules and resources required to carry out these activities.

design reviews and audits of the quality system, processes and/or product shall be carried out by personnel independent of those having direct responsibility for the work being performed.

Comment: We feel that this statement could cause long and acrimonious debates within an organization. The engineer and the manager responsible for the product or process have the primary responsibility for process and product quality and must take part in the reviews and audits. The guideline suggests (and we agree) that an independent reviewer's objectivity would help to ensure the quality of the product or process. Many companies have established an independent quality assurance organization to perform these duties. When there is a disagreement between those with primary responsibility and the independent reviewer, senior management must quickly settle those differences.

Reason: It is an accepted principle in software development that a verification process yields better results when someone in addition to the author of the product verifies the product's quality. For a product, the independent reviewer can be an engineer on the project who has not created the product being reviewed, or an engineer from another project. For auditing a project's engineering process, the independent reviewer can be an engineer or senior manager who is not directly involved with the project.

Means to ensure: The Quality Policy should include the previous statement from the guideline or a similar one. The SPH should detail the Quality Policy's implementation in describing the review and audit processes that occur during product development and maintenance. The SDP should identify the organizations the engineers performing the independent review and audits will come from, so that budgets and schedules for these activities can be identified.

Some companies may create a software process quality assurance organization to perform or take part in these audits. For each project this organization would have a Software Quality Assurance Plan.

4.1.1.2.3 Management Representative

The supplier shall appoint a management representative who, irrespective of

other responsibilities, shall have defined authority and responsibility for ensuring that the requirements of [ISO 9001] are implemented and maintained.

Comment: This section should be given serious consideration by senior management. We feel only a manager with "line" versus "staff" authority can have this responsibility due to the effect any "ensuring" activities that this person performs may have on a project's budget and schedule. Instead of saying "ensuring," which implies direct responsibility for the outcome, the guideline should have said "assuring" if the goal was for senior management to have an objective report concerning the effectiveness of the organization's engineering process.

Reason: One of the basic principles of the guideline is that the requirement for a quality process comes from senior management. Senior management should appoint an individual with direct responsibility and authority to ensure that such a process is established and used during the development and maintenance of the product. This individual must be seen as an instrument of senior management with full backing from senior management from whom he/she derives his/her authority. This individual must have a direct reporting link to senior management or be a member of senior management.

Means to ensure: The Quality Policy should identify the individual by position or title who is responsible for ensuring the existence and use of a documented engineering process. We believe that for this person to be credible, he/she should have an extensive engineering background as well as line (versus staff) management authority. We recommend that the senior engineering manager have this responsibility that is his/hers by the very nature of their position.

4.1.1.3   Management Review

The quality system adopted to satisfy the requirements of [ISO 9001] shall be reviewed at appropriate intervals by the supplier's management to ensure its continuing suitability and effectiveness. Records of such reviews shall be maintained.

Reason: One of the guideline's basic principles is that senior management must be aware of the quality processes (engineering processes) and have a basic level of understanding concerning those processes. In addition, senior management must ensure that the practices and procedures used to support these process are being followed and that they are effective. Far too often senior management puts a process in place but never checks on its implementation or its effectiveness. To ensure that the quality system is effective, there should be regular reviews conducted by senior management so that senior management can act quickly and decisively in the support of a quality process.

Means to ensure: The Quality Policy should state that the SPH is to be regularly reviewed by senior management at least once a year. The Quality Policy should also identify an individual by title or position who is responsible for conducting the management reviews of the SPH with senior management. Records should be kept of the review. The point the guideline is making here is the same point that all the ISO 9000 standards are trying to make. Senior management must be tied into the process that defines and ensures that use of an engineering process within their organization. Senior management should also institute a metrics program and review that program's reports to ensure that the engineering process that the organization is using is meeting the organization's quality goals.

6
Purchaser Management Responsibility

The guideline addresses one of the key problem areas of software development, that is, that purchaser management also has responsibilities in the development of a software product. Basically it should ensure that

> the requirements for the product are explicitly, accurately, and completely stated;

> communication with the supplier concerning questions and proposals are addressed by the right people and in a timely manner; and

> the purchaser organization fulfills its contractual agreements and is prepared to take ownership of the product through the acceptance tests of the product.

In addition, supplier and purchaser management have a shared responsibility to ensure that joint, periodic reviews take place to confirm that both organizations are fulfilling their contractual obligations and that any risk to schedule and product quality is identified and is being managed.

4.1.2 Purchaser's Management Responsibility

The purchaser should cooperate with the supplier to provide all necessary information in a timely manner and resolve pending items.

Comment: Purchaser management often wonders why a supplier fails to deliver a product that meets the purchaser's needs when the purchaser needs it. In many cases the problem is caused by the purchaser's failure to work closely with the supplier during the requirements specification phase.

Reason: The product's requirements, and other information concerning the product, originate from the purchaser. If the purchaser fails to deliver these requirements in a timely and accurate manner, then the product's delivery date, functionality, and quality are at risk.

Means to ensure: The contract between the purchaser and supplier must be specific as to the purchaser's responsibilities and the time frame in which those responsibilities must be met. The supplier's SPH should identify the activities that are required to ensure that the supplier and purchaser are working closely, and these activities should be spelled out in the contract.

The purchaser should assign a representative with the responsibility for dealing with the supplier on contractual matters. This representative should have the authority commensurate with the need to deal with contractual matters which include, but are not limited to, the following:

Reason: Having the supplier taking contractually binding direction from one purchaser representative minimizes the budget and schedule slips that ensue when several purchaser personnel give possibly contradictory direction to the supplier, or the purchaser and supplier fail to update costs and schedules based on the changes required by the purchaser. In actuality the purchaser is likely to have more than one person working with the supplier to identify requirements. What the guideline is driving at here is that only one representative from the purchaser has the authority to approve the requirements or changes to the requirements.

Means to ensure: The purchaser should designate in the contract an individual, by position or title, with the authority and responsibility to conclude agreements with the supplier concerning schedule, cost, and functionality. The guideline suggests that more flexibility than this be allowed (i.e., "commensurate with the need to deal with contractual matters"), but flexibility on this topic should be limited and tightly controlled by the purchaser management.

a) defining the purchaser's requirements to the supplier;

Means to ensure: Identify in the contract the purchaser's representative, by position or title, who approves all requirements or changes to the requirements. In the contract, state that the supplier bears the costs for any work performed in implementing unapproved requirements.

b) answering questions from the supplier;

Reason: The supplier will likely have technical questions during product specification and development. The time required to develop and deliver a product may depend on receiving timely and accurate answers to these questions. There must be a single point of contact in the purchaser's organization to ensure that the supplier's questions are directed to the right person, and that the answers are accurate, complete, and delivered in a timely manner. Eventually informal contacts between the supplier and purchaser will develop. Both purchaser and supplier management should monitor these discussions to ensure that they do not create misunderstandings between the purchaser and the supplier organizations.

Means to ensure: The contract should identify the need for regular technical exchange meetings and an acceptable time frame for answering the supplier's technical questions that arise from these meetings. Minutes of these meetings should be kept and distributed to both parties. The contract should also identify the purchaser and supplier representatives through whom all requests that could impact requirements should be channeled. For the informal discussions that are bound to occur, supplier and purchaser management should be notified when they have occurred and review the content of those discussions.

c) approving the suppliers' proposals;

Reason: Designating one individual in the purchaser organization for approving the supplier's proposals protects both the purchaser and the supplier. The purchaser is protected from a supplier who seeks to add features (and costs) that are not really needed. The supplier is protected from a purchaser that allows several individuals from the purchaser organization to give possible contradictory direction.

Means to ensure: Designate one individual by position and title in the contract who has the authority to approve supplier proposals.

d) concluding agreements with the supplier;

Reason: Only one individual from the purchaser's organization should have the authority to contract with the supplier for goods and services. This ensures that the supplier does not receive conflicting technical direction from the purchaser, which could cause a product to be delivered late, exceed costs, or fail to meet technical requirements.

Means to ensure: The contract should identify the individual from the purchaser's organization with the sole authority to conclude contractually binding agreements with the supplier.

e) ensuring the purchaser's organization observes the agreements made with the supplier;

Reason: The purchaser may be under contractual obligation to the supplier for the delivery of certain products, services, or information. Failure on the part of the purchaser to meet this obligation could cause the supplier to deliver a product that is late or missing functionality. The supplier may rightfully hold the purchaser responsible for any supplier shortfall in performance due to the failure of the purchaser to meet their contractual obligations.

Means to ensure: The contract should identify the activities and their schedule that allow the supplier to ensure that the purchaser is meeting its contractual obligations. These activities could be technical reviews, purchaser status reports, and testing of purchaser products before delivery to the supplier. Purchaser management should review these activities to ensure that its organization is fulfilling the agreements with the supplier.

f) defining acceptance criteria and procedures;

Reason: Acceptance criteria and procedures are the responsibility of the purchaser. These criteria and procedures should be defined, baselined, and delivered by the purchaser to the supplier for review. A review by the supplier is necessary to ensure the agreement by both parties as to the validity of the criteria and procedures. This topic is discussed in section 5.8 of the guideline.

Means to ensure: The purchaser's acceptance plan, which identifies the acceptance test procedures and test cases, should be identified as a contractual deliverable from the purchaser to the supplier. The contract should require that both the purchaser and the supplier agree on the validity of acceptance criteria and procedures before the acceptance tests take place.

g) dealing with the purchaser-supplied software items that are found unsuitable for use.

Reason: The purchaser may be under contract to deliver software items (and hardware) to the supplier for use in the development or maintenance of a product. Both the purchaser and the supplier want to avoid a situation where purchaser-supplied items, which are found unsuitable by the supplier, may impact the development costs and schedule or the functionality of the delivered product.

Means to ensure: The contract should identify which items are to be delivered by the purchaser, which items are to undergo acceptance testing by the supplier, and the process that will be used to resolve any issues the supplier has with purchaser-supplied products. The supplier may want to insert a clause in the contract stating that products that fail the supplier's acceptance test will cause at a minimum a day-to-day slip in schedule until an acceptable product is delivered. The purpose of this clause is to underline the importance of the need for the purchaser to meet its obligations.

4.1.3 Joint Reviews

Regular joint reviews involving the supplier and purchaser should be scheduled to cover the following aspects, as appropriate:

Reason: Joint reviews are needed for a number of reasons. First, they ensure that there is a common understanding between the purchaser and the supplier concerning the product requirements and the manner in which the product is to be validated and tested before acceptance by the purchaser. In addition, although unstated here, joint reviews are needed during the development cycle. Without reviews of the product at intermediate stages, the purchaser risks receiving a system that may not meet the functional or usability requirements, or a product that is delivered late.

Means to ensure: State in the contract that joint reviews should take place at key milestones in the development cycle as well as on a regular basis during the development effort. In the contract, specify the material to be reviewed (e.g., requirements documents, test plans, test cases, user interface design, project status, etc.), the schedule for the review, and the time frame for the delivery of the items to the purchaser before the review. The contract should also outline the manner in which action items arising from the review will be handled and the sign-off process needed to indicate that the action item is complete.

a) conformance of the software to the purchaser's agreed requirements specification;

Comment: A review of the software does not prove or disprove conformance to the purchaser's requirements. A review might be part of that conformance check, but testing the product is really the means by which conformance is determined.

Reason: The supplier derives the detailed software requirements from a high-level System Specification or marketing requirements document and creates a software requirements specification (or functional specification). Opportunities for misunderstandings during this transition are abundant; therefore, a review of the software requirements document by both the supplier and the purchaser is highly recommended. (As mentioned in Chapter 3, the guideline does not address the phase that turns purchaser requirements into detailed software requirements.)

Means to ensure: The contract should require a software requirements review. The contract should state that the supplier's software requirements specification is a deliverable item, and that it must be delivered in advance of the review to allow the purchaser to review the document. During this review, the supplier should be able to show a direct connection from the purchaser's requirements to the detailed requirements as identified by the supplier.

b) verification results; or validation;

Comment: Verification means that an audit, review, or inspection was performed to ensure that stated practices and procedures were followed, although the guideline also includes testing of product components under the heading of verification. Validation, according to the guideline, refers to the formal testing of a complete and integrated product to ensure that it meets functional, technical, and usability requirements.

Reason: The purchaser may require that the supplier's validation (test) and/or verification (process audit) results be delivered to the purchaser for review and approval. This requirement is meant to ensure that the supplier actually engaged in sound engineering practices and procedures during the development and testing of the product.

Means to ensure: The contract should identify verification and validation results as supplier deliverables to the purchaser. In addition, the contract should state the need and schedule for a joint review of these deliverables so that the supplier and purchaser can agree to completeness and accuracy of the material being reviewed.

c) acceptance test results;

Reasons: The purchaser may run acceptance tests before accepting the supplier's product. If these tests fail, the supplier must have the right to review the test cases procedures, results, and manner in which the tests were run. Both the purchaser and supplier must agree that any reported failure was a problem with the product and not a problem caused by the manner in which the product was tested.

Means to ensure: The contract should state that the acceptance test plan, test cases, test procedure, and test results are deliverables to the supplier. The contract should also state that these deliverables are to be delivered several weeks in advance of a joint review to allow time for the supplier to study the deliverables and prepare to discuss with the purchaser any issues the supplier may have.

The results of such reviews should be agreed to and documented.

Reason: The purpose of a joint review is to arrive at a common understanding concerning the items being reviewed. Documenting the results of the review minimizes the risk of disagreements at a later date.

Means to ensure: Document the results of the reviews and distribute the documentation to both supplier and purchaser. The documented results (and the sign-off on these results) should become part of the project documentation.

7

The Supplier's Quality System

Supplier management must first identify the organization's goals when developing a product and then ensure the existence of an engineering environment where these goals can be reached in the most efficient manner possible. This chapter identifies supplier management's responsibility to ensure the existence of an engineering environment that has

defined engineering processes and procedures;

development and maintenance plans based on the defined process and procedures;

reviews, audits, and tests to determine the quality of the product(s) being developed and effectiveness of the process used to develop those products; and

corrective actions based on the information gained form reviews, audits, and tests.

Without an organization-wide understanding and commitment to the engineering process, each engineering project will be left to "muddle through" the best it can, with the consequence that the supplier will likely fail to develop reliable products in a consistent manner.

4.2   Quality System

4.2.1   General

The supplier should establish and maintain a documented quality system. The quality system should be an integrated process throughout the entire life cycle, thus ensuring that quality is being built in as development progresses, rather than being discovered at the end of the process. Problem prevention should be emphasized rather than depending on correction after occurrence.

Comment: This statement speaks to two types of quality: quality in the development process, and a product's quality. The guideline speaks directly not to product quality but to process quality. Engineering organizations can measure their development processes against the guideline to detect gaps that may adversely affect the quality of the product.

Reason: Product quality (in the sense that a product meets its functional, technical, and usability goals) can be gained from the use of an engineering process in the development and maintenance of a product. The quality system is a documented engineering process that identifies the steps followed in the development of a product, the practices and procedures used to support those steps, the roles and responsibilities of the organizations and individuals within the process, and a continuous check of the process and product's quality during each step of the development phase.

Means to ensure: The Quality Policy should dictate that the organization follow a defined engineering process in the development and maintenance of all software products. A software process handbook (SPH) should document the engineering process. Senior management must ensure that appropriate staff is involved in the development of the SPH (e.g., project managers, senior software, test, and configuration-management engineers).

The supplier should ensure the effective implementation of the documented quality system.

Reason: It is the responsibility of the supplier management to ensure that any systems, process, and procedures put in place are followed and are effective. Too often management dictates the use practices and procedures but fails to ensure that they are being used and are effective.

Means to ensure: The Quality Policy should state that supplier management hold regular reviews to ensure the use and effectiveness of the practices and procedures that have been put in place for use in the development and maintenance of products. Minutes of these reviews should be kept, and action items assigned with a date for completion. Follow-up reviews should take place to ensure that any changes to practices and procedures are effective.

The Quality Policy should identify that independent audits of the engineering process are to be performed. A plan should be created that identifies the activities and resources required to perform those audits. Senior management would review the results of those audits and act accordingly.

4.2.2   Quality System Documentation

All the quality system elements, requirements and provisions should be clearly documented in a systematic and orderly manner.

Reason: The SPH is a concise definition of an engineering process and the roles and responsibilities of the individuals in that process. The SPH should be read and understood by all parties involved in the development or maintenance of a product. From this understanding can evolve the teamwork required to produce or maintain a product in the most rapid and cost-effective manner possible.

Means to ensure: The SPH should identify the phases, steps, practices, and procedures that make up the engineering process used to create or maintain a product. The SPH identifies the roles and responsibilities of the various organizations within that process and the control mechanisms used to ensure the process is functioning appropriately.

The SPH identifies the system life-cycle phases, development procedures, testing procedures, quality control activity procedures, configuration management, change control procedures, and document control. In addition, the roles and responsibilities of the personnel involved in each life-cycle phase should be defined in the SPH. Also, each phase should have clearly identified entry and exit criteria. The SPH should have specification or documentation templates to support all the engineering processes identified in the SPH.

The SPH should be the guiding document for the engineering process. Its location and content should be known by all personnel involved with that process.

4.2.3   Quality Plan

The supplier should prepare and document a quality plan to implement quality activities for each software development on the basis of the quality system, and ensure that it is understood and observed by the organizations concerned.

Comment: Readers are already aware of our criticism of this section. The quality plan as defined in this section overlaps several of the other documented engineering processes and development plans. An organization will have a defined engineering process (SPH), software development plans for each project (SDP), configuration management plans (CMP) for each product, and documentation plans for each project and product. We feel that the quality plan should describe a plan to implement an organization's documented (in the SPH) quality assurance activities such as audits, inspections, and metrics for product and process improvements for a particular product.

Reason: The SDP lays out the costs, budget, and schedules needed to implement the quality system, the defined engineering process found in the SPH, for a specific project or product. The quality plan should identify the activities, schedule, and resources needed to perform the "value added" activities that ensure the implementation of the engineering processes needed to develop or maintain the product (i.e., audits and inspections).

Means to ensure: The supplier's Quality Policy should state that the SPH is to be used as on all projects and that a project's SDP, which details the project's costs and schedules required to implement the engineering process, is to be based on the use of the SPH. The quality plan should identify the activities, resources, and schedules needed to ensure the implementation of the SPH on the specific project. The quality plan could be a subordinate plan to the SDP or a stand-alone plan. The quality plan should identify the resources required for audits and inspections, what will be audited and inspected, and when these audits and inspections are to take place. In addition, the quality plan should describe the outputs of these activities, how they will be used, and how they will be stored and maintained.

4.3   Internal Quality System Audits

Internal quality audits

The supplier shall carry out a comprehensive system of planned and documented internal quality [system] audits to verify whether quality activities comply with planned arrangements and to determine the effectiveness of the quality system.

Reason: This section can and should be read in two different ways. Reviews, walk-throughs, and configuration management are "audits" to ensure that "quality activities" like design, code, and tests are effective parts of the "quality system" or the engineering process. In addition, audits of the "audits" should be performed to ensure that the reviews, walk-throughs, and configuration management are indeed taking place, that documented procedures are being followed, and that the reviews, walk-throughs, configuration management, and their respective procedures are effective.

Means to ensure: The Quality Policy should identify reviews and audits as part of the engineering process. The SPH defines reviews, tests, and configuration control as part of the engineering process. In addition the SPH calls for audits of these processes to ensure that they are taking place. The quality plan identifies the schedule and costs associated with these reviews and audits. The quality plan should identify

what will be audited,

who will conduct the audits,

what is the audit schedule,

what resources will be required to perform the audit or aid in the audit,

how the results of the audits will be conveyed,

who will be the recipient of the results of the audit reports,

what records of the audit will be kept,

what are the prerequisites of the audit, and

what are the exit criteria for the audit.

These audits should be performed by individuals independent of the organization being audited.

Audits shall be scheduled on the basis of the status and importance of the activity.

Reason: Audits are part of an engineering process and should be planned to ensure they take place, are properly focused, and are part of an integrated engineering effort as opposed to being disruptive to the flow of the engineering process or curtailed due to budget or schedule constraints.

Means to ensure: The requirement for reviews, tests, configuration control, and the audits of these processes are spelled out in the Quality Policy. The SPH defines how these activities are implemented. The quality plan details budgets and schedules for these audits and inspections, while configuration control and testing will most likely have their own separate plans that are subordinate to or part of the SDP. Documented proof that these activities took place should become part of the project documentation (to include quality records).

The audits and follow-up actions shall be carried out in accordance with documented procedures.

Reason: Audits should be performed in an engineering and business-like manner in order to reap full benefit from the time and resources spent on the audit activities. To avoid time-consuming discussions concerning the appropriate approach for performing audits, the approach should be documented in the quality plan and agreed to by those performing the audit as well as by those being audited before the audit takes place.

Means to ensure: The SPH should describe the manner in which audits and inspections take place and provide for documentation templates to support those efforts. Senior management should ensure that members of the staff are trained in conducting audits and inspections. Senior management should ensure that all members of the engineering staff understand the benefits of such activities. The quality assurance plan identifies the schedule and resources required to implement inspections and audits and the detailed implementation of the audit and inspection process identified in the SPH.

The results of the audits shall be documented and brought to the attention of the personnel having responsibility in the area audited. The management personnel responsible for the area shall take timely corrective action on the deficiencies found by the audit.

Comment: The first step before any "corrective action" is taken based on the results of the audit is for the organization as a whole (i.e., auditors, audited area, and management) to agree on the results of the audit and the corrective action to be taken.

Reason: There needs to be a closed-loop management process in place to ensure that the deficiencies discovered during an audit or inspection are reviewed and that steps are initiated by management to address the root cause of the deficiency.

Means to ensure: The SPH should define a process that requires some level of management above project management to review all audit and inspection reports. The SPH should identify the organizations that are to respond to problems identified in audits or reviews. The Software Quality Assurance Plan should identify the schedule for senior management's reviews of the results of the audits.

4.4 Corrective Action

The supplier shall establish, document and maintain procedures for . . .

Comment: In this section the guideline is pointing out the need for a closed-loop management process. It's not enough to detect and correct instances of nonconformance. An engineering organization should be analyzing its own performance and adjust its practices and procedures based on the results of that analysis rather than just applying temporary solutions to recurring problems.

a) investigating the cause of nonconforming product and the corrective action needed to prevent recurrence;

Reason: Within an engineering process there are procedures (e.g., reviews, audits, inspections, tests) to detect when a product or component suffers from nonconformance. Detection is only one part of the process needed to deal with nonconformance; prevention is the other part. Without addressing the cause of nonconformance, there is no guarantee that the nonconformance will not occur again and have a negative impact on schedule and usability.

Means to ensure: There must be a conscious, managed, structured process for investigating and preventing recurrence of nonconformance. The Quality Policy should state that the engineering process as defined in the SPH shall describe this investigation and prevention process. The SDP and Software Quality Assurance Plan identify the costs, schedules, and reviews of that investigative and preventive process.

b) analyzing all processes, work operations, concessions, quality records, service reports and customer complaints to detect and eliminate potential causes of nonconforming product;

Reason: Information from many sources is available to engineering management that can be used to determine the cause of nonconformance. Service reports (from field engineers and help-desk engineers) and customer complaints often go overlooked by the developers or are not part of the evaluation.

Means to ensure: The Quality Policy should identify the need for review of information concerning instances of product nonconformity from all sources. The SPH should define a cross-organizational review process to include the roles and responsibilities of the various organizations involved in the process. An organization-wide (as opposed to any specific project or product) Software Quality Assurance Plan identifies the budget and schedule for the activities required to implement the process.

c) initiating preventive actions to deal with problems to a level corresponding to the risk encountered;

Reason: This section points out the need to take action once an analysis of a given problem has been performed. Too often organizations suffer from "analysis paralysis" and fail to take action.

Means to ensure: Once the problem review process has identified the root cause of the problem and a likely solution, it is imperative that an individual be made responsible for implementing the solution. We have found that assigning an AR (action request) to an individual (rather than to a group) with a date for when the AR is to be complete coupled with a regular review of all open AR(s) is an effective means for ensuring that preventive measures are initiated. The guideline, interestingly enough, points out that a certain amount of digression is to be used when applying the preventive action based on the risk involved. In other words, be careful not to use an elephant gun to kill a mosquito.

d) applying controls to ensure that corrective actions are taken and that they are effective;

Reason: A problem is not corrected just by initiating a corrective action. It is necessary to manage the implementation of the action to ensure that the corrective actions bring about the desired results.

Means to ensure: The SPH should describe a generic control process. In most cases the definition of the configuration management process would suffice for an individual project or product. The SDP identifies the schedule and budget required to implement the control activities or refers to a subordinate configuration management plan (CMP). The software quality plan should identify the manner in which discovery of nonconformance through the audit and inspection procedures will be transmitted to the project managers responsible for ensuring that there are no further instances of nonconformance.

e) implementing and recording changes in procedures resulting from corrective action.

Reason: Not all instances of nonconformance result from individuals' failing to perform in a flawless manner. In some case, the engineering procedures (to include audits and inspections) may be faulty. A corrective action may require a change in a processes or procedures.

Means to ensure: The Quality Policy should state that changes to the engineering process defined in the SPH may be required. The Quality Policy should state that changes to procedures must be reviewed and authorized by the individual identified in the Quality Policy as being responsible for the engineering process as documented in the SPH. The SPH should identify the process by which changes can be recommended, approved, and distributed.

8

The Purchaser and Supplier Contract

This is a very important stage. In the rush to get "on contract" and develop a sense of trust and good fellowship between the two organizations, many difficult issues are glossed over and procedures needed to deal with the problems that are sure to arise during the development effort are not defined. Basically, the lack of an engineering approach in dealing with business relationships at the very beginning of a project increases the likelihood of product budget, schedule, and quality issues. For the short-term feeling of "teamwork" and the warm feeling the effort is under way, both the purchaser and supplier have put the future at risk.

The purchaser and supplier must come to an agreement on contractual obligations and identify methods for resolving contract issues that may arise between the purchaser and supplier. Both supplier and purchaser management must

understand the scope of the contract,

agree on its organization's responsibilities,

identify and plan to minimize risks (e.g., schedule, budget, legal),

agree to the terminology used in the contract,

identify a process to handle changes to requirements, and

agree on the process for handling bugs found in the product delivered by the supplier.

Expanding the scope of the guideline, which we recommend, the above comments apply to an organization's marketing (purchaser) and engineering (supplier) groups.

Comment: Section 5 of the guideline addresses the heart of the software engineering effort. Cumulatively it addresses the planning, implementation, and testing of the product by the supplier and purchaser's acceptance testing. We have divided this section into several chapters, but we need to briefly address section 5.1, a section general in nature, in this chapter before we begin our discussion of the other subsections.

5   Quality System—Life-Cycle Activities

5.1   General

A software development project should be organized according to a life-cycle model. Quality-related activities should be planned and implemented with respect to the nature of the life-cycle model used.

This part of ISO 9000 is intended for application irrespective of the life-cycle model used. Should any description, guidance, requirement or structure be read differently, this is unintended and should not be read as indicating that the requirement or guidance is restricted to a specific life-cycle model only.

Comment: Section 5.1 is really a disclaimer. The guideline states that all development projects (and maintenance projects) should follow an organized life-cycle (or process). The disclaimer is that nothing in the guideline requires or implies that any specific life cycle be followed. Suppliers are free to use any life cycle they deem best suited for the type of product being developed or maintained, as long as consideration is given to the various activities referred to in Sections 5.2 through 5.10 as life-cycle activities. These activities are the basic activities found in a managed software process.

Software engineering has commonly accepted practices and procedures. Within software engineering, there are several similar product life cycles that lay out a step-by-step process, often iterative, that takes a product through specification, analysis, design, implementation, test, and maintenance. Examples are the classic Waterfall and the more flexible Spiral, Evolutionary, and Incremental life cycles. The guideline does not dictate a particular life cycle, but it does require that a life cycle be identified by the supplier and used to develop and maintain software. A different life cycle can be used and tailored from one project or product to another, but there must be a life cycle used.

5.2   Contract Review

5.2.1   General

The supplier should establish and maintain procedures for contract review and for the coordination of these activities.

Comment: The previous sentence speaks only to the supplier but it should also apply to the purchaser. Purchaser managers reading this section should take steps to ensure that their organization is prepared to meet the goals identified in this section of the guideline.

Reason: Many software development projects end in failure or exceed original cost and schedule estimates when the purchaser and the supplier mistakenly believe that they agree on requirements or when either or both the purchaser and supplier organizations do not fully realize the level of commitment required to meet their respective contractual obligations.

Means to ensure: The supplier's management should identify the key contract negotiators. Minutes of contract meetings must be kept, and review of those minutes must take place by management within both organizations. Also, the supplier's management must see to it that the contract is reviewed internally to ensure the various supplier's organizations (e.g., developers, testers, technical writers) have a consistent understanding of what will be expected from them. This internal review process should be identified in the SPH as one of the engineering steps.

a) The scope of the contract and requirements are defined and documented;

Reason: Disagreements, sometime acrimonious, can occur between the purchaser and the supplier when the scope of the contract and requirements are not clearly stated or when "implied" product requirements are not met. The first step in the project is to ensure that both the purchaser and the supplier have a common understanding of requirements, deliverables, schedules, and interactions between the purchaser and supplier during and after the product is developed. Implied requirements do not exist and are not contractually binding.

Means to ensure: There are two documents used to detail the technical requirements of a software product and other project or product deliverables, the System Specification and the Statement of Work (SOW). The System Specification (sometimes known as the Marketing Requirements Document or Customer Requirements Document) is a high-level technical description of the product to be built and defines the purchaser's requirements. It addresses such topics as functionality, external inputs/outputs, technical constraints product, and system configuration.

The contract may also require certain other deliverables or activities, which are sometimes described in a separate document, the Statement of Work (SOW). Topics addressed in the SOW could include supplier documentation, formal purchaser/supplier reviews, and development status reports and other activities that describe the general interactions between the purchaser and the supplier.

b) possible contingencies or risks are identified;

Reason: Senior management is often unaware of the technical, schedule, or budget risks involved with software projects for which senior management is ultimately responsible, and yet it is that level of management that can obtain the resources to minimize the risks. Product development and maintenance risks must be identified to senior management in quantifiable terms related to budget and schedule so that senior management can make the proper business decisions needed to minimize these risks.

Means to ensure: First, the supplier's management must review and authorize the System Specification and Statement of Work. Second, the supplier's management should request a risk management plan from the project and product managers (i.e., engineering and marketing) that identifies the assumptions made concerning the proposed work, the risks involved, and the plan to minimize the risks. This process needs to be identified in the SPH.

c) proprietary information is adequately protected;

Reason: Sometimes, purchasers believe they have paid for all materials involved in the creation and production of a product. The purchaser and supplier must agree on who owns items like source code, algorithms, design, resale rights, and so on.

Means to ensure: The contract should clearly state what ownership rights the purchaser has concerning the product being produced and identify by name those items that the supplier has developed that are to be considered the sole property of the purchaser.

d) any requirements differing from those in the tender are resolved;

Comment: The term "tender" is defined in ISO 9001 as "Offer made by a supplier in response to an invitation to satisfy a contract award to provide product."

Reason: A development effort starts with a Marketing Requirements Document/System Specification stating high-level technical requirements (a tender). The supplier may respond to the purchaser by creating a more detailed document describing the software and hardware required to fulfill those requirements. The supplier's response should be reviewed by the purchaser to ensure that it addresses all the purchaser's requirements and not a subset or superset of the requirements.

Means to ensure: The supplier's SPH should state as a precursor to signing any contract that the supplier and purchaser must agree to the purchaser's requirements and the costs and schedule required to meet those requirements. Where the supplier does create a more detailed statement of software and hardware requirements, those requirements should be traced back to one or more purchaser requirements.

e) the supplier has the capability to meet contractual requirements;

Reason: The purchaser is interested in the supplier's capabilities to develop a product that meets the purchaser's requirements. This is really the intent of the ISO 9001 certification process, to allow the purchaser to gain some level of confidence in a supplier's engineering capabilities. The purchaser should also determine whether the supplier has the personnel with the technical and application-specific skills to meet the contractual requirement.

Means to ensure: In the contract, the purchaser should require a review of the supplier's software engineering process and the documentation that shows the process is used in the development of software products. The purchaser should also ask for a brief technical résumé of the key technical personnel that the supplier intends to use on the project. With the exception of a staff member leaving the supplier's employment, the supplier must ensure that these people will fulfill the project-specific effort for which they have been considered. In addition the purchaser should request from the supplier details of previous supplier projects similar in nature to the one being considered by the purchaser.

f) the supplier's responsibility with regard to subcontracted work is defined;

Comment: See section 6.7 for more details concerning this topic.

Reason: The supplier may subcontract part of the development work. Poor-quality work performed by a subcontractor has just as much negative effect on a product as poor-quality work performed by the supplier.

Means to ensure: In the contract the purchaser should state that subcontractors to the supplier need to have a defined engineering process and that the supplier is responsible for auditing the subcontractor's capability, with a review of the audit to be performed by the purchaser. Basically, the supplier should take the same view of a subcontractor that the purchaser takes of the supplier.

g) the terminology is agreed by both parties;

Reason: During contract development and through the initial stages of product specification and analysis, the terms used to describe the product are in the language of the purchaser, and not necessarily that of the supplier. This can cause misconceptions as different terms are used for the same object or the supplier has an incomplete understanding of the terminology.

Means to ensure: A dictionary of terms should be kept for each development project. Such a dictionary helps during the contract/specification stage, as both the purchaser and supplier work toward agreement upon terms and conditions. In addition, the dictionary shortens the learning curve for new people coming on board the project during the development stage.

h) the purchaser has the capability to meet contractual obligations.

Reason: The purchaser may be on contract to deliver specifications, hardware, software, and facilities for use by the supplier. The supplier's management must review the purchaser's capability to meet these obligations and ensure that there are contractual safeguards protecting the supplier from failure on the purchaser's part to meet its contractual obligations.

Means to ensure: In the contract, ensure that purchaser obligations, a schedule for meeting the obligations, and key individuals in the purchaser's organization who are responsible for delivery of contracted items or services are identified. Supplier management should review purchaser plans for meeting its contractual obligations. The supplier's management should require the status of these deliverables on a regular basis. In effect, when the purchaser has obligations for supplying the supplier with the facilities, products, or services, the roles of the purchaser and supplier have been, to a certain degree, reversed.

Records of such contract reviews should be maintained.

Reason: During the contract reviews agreements and changes to the contract may be suggested and agreed to by both purchaser and supplier. If these agreements and changes are not captured in writing, there exists the possibility that they will not be incorporated in the final contract.

Means to ensure: At the end of each contract review a summary of the discussion and agreements should be made. After the contract review has taken place a documented record of the review should be created and sent to both supplier and purchaser. This document should be reviewed and signed by both parties, and copies should be maintained by both the supplier and purchaser.

5.2.2   Contract Items on Quality

Among others, the following items are frequently found to be relevant in the contract:

Comment: This is an example of the guideline as a guideline, not a rule. The guideline does not dictate that any of the following need be in a contract, nor does it preclude the possibility of other items being included in the contract. The following sections identify important considerations and it would be a good idea to address them in the contract.

a) acceptance criteria;

Comment: Acceptance testing is the final stage of product testing. The purchaser develops acceptance test cases to show that the product meets the functional and performance requirements in an operational environment.

Reason: Many times the purchaser is unprepared to accept the product or has created invalid test cases upon which the acceptance decision will be based. The supplier benefits when the purchaser defines the acceptance criteria, for two reasons. First, it shows that the purchaser is committed to taking ownership of the product and has thought through the necessary steps to accept and use the product, thus reducing the burden on the supplier, who sometimes must support the acceptance testing process. Second, it ensures that the supplier and purchaser have an agreed-upon set of criteria for acceptance that avoids arguments over whether the acceptance test was valid or if there is a problem with the product. Arguments such as these can prolong the supplier's involvement beyond the supplier's original schedule and budget.

Means to ensure: The purchaser should have an acceptance plan that identifies test cases, test case description, test environment, and schedule. The supplier should review the acceptance test cases for accuracy. The acceptance test cases should be identified in the contract as a purchaser deliverable to the supplier. In cases where this is not made part of the contract it must be identified to the supplier management as a risk.

b) handling of changes in purchaser's requirements during the development;

Reason: Changes to requirements are a normal event during the product life cycle and occur from the moment the original requirements are agreed to by the purchaser and supplier through development and until the time that the product is no longer used by the purchaser or supported by the supplier. Projects are usually late or over budget not only for technical reasons but also when budgets and schedules are not updated to reflect changes in the requirements.

Means to ensure: The contract should identify purchaser and supplier representatives who have authority to approve changes to the requirements. The supplier's SPH should identify the configuration control process to be used during product development or maintenance that will support the handling of changes to the requirements (see section 6.1, Configuration Control). The SDP (or the configuration management plan) identifies the budget and schedules required to implement the process.

c) handling of problems detected after acceptance, including quality-related claims and purchaser complaints;

Reason: Almost all software products contain latent errors (bugs) that become apparent only after the purchaser has accepted the product. There may also be issues with regard to product usability that arise once the product has been put into use.

Means to ensure: The purchaser and the supplier should agree to a support plan once the product is delivered. A support plan is meant to ensure that supplier resources needed to handle problems after acceptance of the product by the purchaser are available and that the time frame for solving problems is agreeable to both the supplier and the purchaser.

The purchaser should review the supplier's field service, help desk, and maintenance engineering capabilities and processes to determine the supplier's capability for supporting a product after delivery.

The supplier should have procedures for handling the following:

bug reporting—help desk, supplier's customer service;

bug tracking—automated tools, manual paperwork flow;

bug prioritizing and processing—configuration control board;

regression testing—subset of system testing; and

version control—release to customer.

These topics are addressed in more detail in section 5.10, Maintenance, and section 6.1, Configuration Management.

d) activities carried out by the purchaser, especially the purchaser's role in requirements specification, installation and acceptance;

Comment: This may be the most important aspect of the guideline. Possibly the prime cause for a product's success or failure in meeting its technical, budget, and schedule goals is the degree of participation by the purchaser in the product's specification, installation, and acceptance.

Reason: The supplier should ensure that the purchaser takes an active role in identifying the requirements and committing to this role and the requirements via contract. In addition, the supplier should also ensure that the purchaser is ready to test and install the product. In many instances the purchaser fails to assume the responsibility for specifying the product's requirements or is ill-prepared to accept, test, and install the product. When such a situation arises, the supplier becomes tied down beyond the scheduled end date, supporting a purchaser who has failed to plan or prepare properly for acceptance, installation, and proliferation of the purchased product.

Means to ensure: The contract should clearly identify the roles and responsibilities for both the purchaser and supplier during the requirement specification and acceptance testing phases. These clauses should identify key people from both purchaser and supplier organizations that are to work together to ensure that the product is specified, installed, and acceptance tested correctly. Timetables for meetings and deliverables that relate to these activities should be identified in the contract. Finally, a strong contractual statement should be made that the supplier is to be compensated for time and effort spent because of the purchaser's failure to perform or prepare for these activities.

e) facilities, tools and software items to be provided by the purchaser;

Reason: The purchaser may need to provide facilities, tools, and software items for use by the supplier in developing the product. Failure to identify the type, quantity, and delivery date of these items could cause budget and schedule overruns.

Means to ensure: In the contract the purchaser's responsibilities for delivery of development facilities, tools, and software should be clearly spelled out by name, version, and date for delivery.

f) standards and procedures to be used;

Reason: The contract may spell out the development guideline and procedures to be used in the development and testing of the product, especially if there are industry guidelines such as there are in some regulated industries (or the ISO 9000 standards). In addition, the purchaser may want to review the supplier's internal procedures (SPH) and ensure, via contract, that these procedures are used during product development.

Means to ensure: Identify in the contract the standards and procedures that are to be used in the development of the product.

g) replication requirements.

Reason: The purchaser may be expecting the supplier to create and deliver more than one copy of the product for more than one release of that product.

Means to ensure: Explicitly state in the contract the replication requirements. The purchaser needs to identify the number of copies of the product, the medium by which the product is delivered, and how many times the supplier is required to release the product.

9

Identify the Purchaser's Requirements

This chapter discusses the need to identify in detail the product's functional, interface, and technical (e.g., performance, safety, reliability, testability, usability, etc.), requirements. Both the purchaser and supplier have a responsibility to ensure these requirements are complete and quantifiable before product development begins. The key to this effort is that the purchaser must take an active role in the identification of the requirements. Another key point is that both organizations must ensure that all requirements are reviewed and jointly agreed to and that approval authority of requirements and proposals is strictly limited to select individuals within both organizations.

5.3 Purchaser's Requirements Specification

5.3.1 General

In order to proceed with software development, the supplier should have a complete, unambiguous set of functional requirements. In addition, these requirements should include all aspects necessary to satisfy the purchaser's need. These may include, but are not limited to, the following: performance, safety, reliability, security and privacy. These requirements should be stated precisely enough so as to allow validation during product acceptance.

Comment: Rarely can a "complete, unambiguous set of functional requirements" be obtained before a project of any significant size can begin. What can be gained at this point is an unambiguous set of high-level requirements with a caveat acknowledged by both parties that the requirements may not be complete and are subject to change. The vehicle for this statement of requirements is the purchaser's requirements specification (also known as Marketing Requirements Document, Customer Requirements Document, or System Specification). The development life cycle chosen (e.g., Waterfall, Spiral, Evolutionary, Phased, etc.) and the degree of prototyping used to develop the product will be based on the accuracy, completeness, and level of understanding concerning the purchaser's requirements.

The purchaser's requirements specification records these requirements. In some cases, this document is provided by the purchaser. If not, the supplier should develop these requirements in close cooperation with the purchaser, and the supplier should obtain the purchaser's approval before entering the development stage. The purchaser's requirements specification should be subject to documentation control and configuration management as part of the development documentation.

Reason: The purchaser and the supplier need a written specification describing the product's functional and performance requirements. This is normally the responsibility of the purchaser. The supplier should make every effort to see that the purchaser fulfills this duty. In the instances where the purchaser is unable to perform this duty, the supplier should create such a document and obtain the purchaser's agreement to the completeness and correctness of the document's contents. The purchaser should understand that the contents of the document will be contractually binding and that the cost of changes to the requirements stated in the specification will be borne by the purchaser.

Means to ensure: The software process handbook (SPH) should identify this requirement definition step as one of the engineering activities that occur during product development. The SPH should have specification templates to support this effort. In addition, the SPH should identify the need for reviews of the purchaser's requirements as embodied in the System Specification. The software development plan (SDP) should identify the schedule and budget required to support this specification and review process.

All interfaces between the software product and other software or hardware products should be fully specified, either directly or by reference, in the purchaser's requirements specification.

Reason: A software product is likely to be part of a larger system. These interfaces are contractually binding since changes to the interface generally have a severe impact on cost, budget, and schedule. The further into the development effort that these interfaces are allowed to change the greater the impact on cost, budget, and schedule.

Means to ensure: A section in the System Specification and the contract should identify the third-party products (by name and version numbers) with which the product to be developed must interface and must reference their technical documentation.

5.3.2 Mutual Cooperation

During the development of the purchaser's requirements specification, attention to the following issues is recommended:

Comment: Far too often, the purchaser and supplier fail to work together to identify the requirements of the system. This causes misunderstandings that will likely result in time-consuming, expensive, and iterative review cycles of the product specification and contract. These iterations slow down the development process and extend the overall time required to bring a product to market.

a) assignment of persons (on both sides) responsible for establishing the purchaser's requirements specification;

Reason: Many times, a purchaser's requirements specification is "tossed over the wall" to the supplier with little realization on the part of the purchaser of what the supplier needs to be stated in the document. The supplier should help the purchaser to provide the type of information at the level of detail needed by the supplier in order to begin the analysis and design.

Means to ensure: Identify key individuals within each organization, and plan for the time and budget necessary to establish the purchaser's requirements. The SPH should have a template for the purchaser's requirements specification that can be used to focus the efforts of both the purchaser and supplier during requirements gathering.

b) methods for agreeing on requirements and approving changes;

Reason: This is possibly the most difficult stage in the development process. Communication content is high; the purchaser may have a somewhat nebulous concept of the requirements; the supplier may be unfamiliar with the purchaser, product application, and operational environment. Requirements specified early in this stage may need to be changed during the course of analysis and later during product development. These changes cannot be unilateral. Both the purchaser and supplier must agree to the scope and costs of the change as well as who will bear the costs of the changes.

Means to ensure: The contract should identify the individuals from both the purchaser and supplier organization responsible for agreeing to the requirements. The supplier and the purchaser should agree upon a specification template to be used to request changes to requirements. Using a template reduces the confusion concerning what information needs to be specified and allows for easier review of that information. A configuration control board (see section 6.1, Configuration Management) made up of representatives from both organizations should meet on a regular basis to review and approve changes to the requirements or any other baseline (software modules, test cases, external interfaces). The supplier's SPH should define this process and the supporting templates. The SDP, or configuration management plan, should identify the budgets and schedules needed to support this process.

c) efforts to prevent misunderstandings such as definition of terms, explanations of background of requirements;

Reason: The supplier may not have the same depth of understanding as the purchaser concerning the application for which the product is being developed. The supplier's learning curve, product quality, and scheduled delivery date is impacted by misunderstandings, or incomplete understanding, of the terminology used to define the requirements and quality records.

The supplier must understand the background of the requirement to ensure that what is being stated as a requirement is truly a requirement and not a design issue that can be met procedurally by the user rather than by the product being developed. Additionally, although all requirements need to be met, some requirements have a greater impact on the product's functionality and usefulness. These should be identified so that the supplier pays particular attention to them during development and test.

Means to ensure: Keep a dictionary of terms used by the purchaser in describing the product. The supplier should work with the purchaser to write the purchaser's product specification, keeping in mind that the purchaser is ultimately responsible for the correctness of the specification. Each requirement should be prioritized by the purchaser and categorized, for example, as critical, essential, and "nice to have."

d) recording and reviewing discussion results on both sides.

Reason: Meetings between the supplier and the purchaser to discuss requirements may go on for some time with requirements being changed and action items being assigned. Documenting the minutes of these meetings and getting the supplier and purchaser management to review the minutes and agreements help avoid misunderstandings both between and within the purchaser and supplier organizations.

Means to ensure: Identify and distribute meeting agendas before the meeting, keep minutes of the meeting, seek for explicit statements of requirements and intent, document agreements, assign action items, distribute minutes after the meeting, maintain minutes under some form of document control, review minutes of prior meetings at the beginning of a new meeting, and track action items to conclusion. These minutes and records should become part of the permanent product documentation.

10
Development Planning

Once a purchaser's requirements have been identified there needs to be a development plan to deliver a product that meets those requirements. The development plan identifies the resources and schedule required to develop a product. The resources and schedule are based on a combination of the purchaser's requirements, engineering practices and procedures used by the supplier to meet those requirements, historical data from previous projects, and the date the purchaser requires the product.

While the software process handbook (SPH) defines the phases of development and the generic inputs and outputs to each phase, the development plan shows how the phases will be implemented and explicitly identifies

the inputs and outputs to each phase,

schedule and resources for each phase,

progress control and status methods,

tools and methods to be used, and

verification procedures for each phase (reviews, audits, and testing).

There are a number of plans that identify the various aspects of the product development, and maintenance, activities. There may be separate plans for development (i.e., analysis, design, and code), testing (functional, integration, and system), configuration management, documentation, and process quality assurance. Whether they are one integrated plan or several, they all should identify these basis elements.

5.4   Development Planning

5.4.1   General

The development plan should cover the following:

Comment: Many development efforts are unplanned, or the planning is at such a level as to be practically useless. Too often, what occurs is "ready, fire, aim." Before planning (budget and schedules) can take place, there must be a clear definition of the goal of the work (product requirements to be met) and the engineering process to be used to perform the work.

a) the definition of the project, including a statement of its objectives and with reference to related purchaser or supplier projects;

Reason: This high-level statement allows the various levels of supplier management to have a consistent and organization-wide understanding of the project's goals and impact on the supplier organization. Without this understanding, resources may be misallocated for this project or other projects both before and during the development effort.

Means to ensure: The SPH should define a template for the software development plan (SDP). The first section of the plan should describe the project and its objectives in a short, clear statement that can be read and understood by all the various organizations and levels of management involved in or responsible for the development of the product. A review of this plan is required by both project and organization-level management.

b) the organization of the project resources, including the team structure, responsibilities, use of sub-contractors and material resources to be used;

Reason: Many times, a project begins without a clear definition of the roles and responsibilities of the various organizations that perform the project's tasks. In addition, clear lines of control and communication are often missing or ill-defined. Without a framework of defined roles, responsibilities, control, and communication, the project participants will likely work at cross-purposes, with a negative impact on the schedule, budget, and costs. When there is no clear organization or definition of roles and responsibilities many hours are spent in meetings rather than developing the product.

Many times, a supplier fails to manage its subcontractors properly. The supplier must ensure that the subcontractor's efforts are successfully integrated into the supplier's efforts and the subcontractor's products have been successfully and seamlessly integrated into the final product delivered to the purchaser.

Means to ensure: The SPH defines the engineering process to be used in the development or maintenance of the product. This definition also includes the roles and responsibilities of the team assembled to develop or maintain the product. The SDP should be based on the SPH. The SDP should be reviewed by senior supplier management since project participants are likely to come from more than one supplier organization.

A supplier should control the activities of a subcontractor in the same manner that the purchaser deals with the supplier. The supplier and subcontractor should agree on requirements, schedules, budgets, and the quality activities that both parties will engage in to ensure the delivery of a product within schedule. The purchaser should review these agreements to ensure that the supplier is qualifying the work being performed by the subcontractor.

Although an organization may have a defined engineering process that project resource plans are based on, each project must also identify the material requirements necessary to develop the product. Examples of these requirements are physical facilities, hardware, and software.

c) development phases (as defined in 5.4.2.1);

Reason: No matter what life-cycle approach a project takes, the development cycle goes through analysis, design, code, and test phases, in that order. The cycle may be Waterfall, Incremental, Iterative, Spiral, or just plain chaotic, but the order is always the same no matter which life cycle is chosen. Even if the most insightful and rapid prototype springs directly into the marketplace, it still will have gone through some level of analysis, design, code, and test. The intent here is to ensure that the supplier organization has an engineering process in place for development, enhancement, or maintenance of a product and bases its plans upon such a process. Ideally, an organization will be flexible and intelligent enough to chose the right life cycle for the project at hand.

Means to ensure: The supplier's Quality Policy should dictate that the SDP is based upon a defined and documented engineering process. The SPH defines this process. The SDP identifies the budget and schedule required to implement the process used to meet the purchaser's requirements. The supplier's management should review the SDP to ensure that the plan reflects the defined process and that the resource estimates for completing the project are reasonable with respect to the purchaser's requirements and the engineering process.

d) the project schedule identifying the tasks to be performed, the resources and time required for each and any interrelationships between tasks;

Reason: Software development goes through distinct phases (analysis, design, code, and test). Within each phase there are a number of tasks that need to be performed. A task has an input from a previous task and its outputs are input to the next task. Once the task's requirements are identified along with the task's inputs and outputs, then a schedule and budget can be determined for each task. The schedule and budget for the various tasks can be rolled up into a project schedule.

Means to ensure: Base the software project schedule and budget on the SPH, the purchaser's requirements, historical data from previous projects, and limited prototype efforts. There should be a documented basis of estimates for budgets and schedules for each task identified in the SPH. The following is an example of a basis of estimate for design.

Basis of Estimate for Design

The following estimates are based on an analysis of the purchaser's requirements, previous projects productivity rates, and the software engineering process. Previous projects have shown that a module averages 400 SLOCS:

1.   Design 40,000 SLOCS
        40,000 SLOCS = 100 design units
        1 unit per person every 1 day = 100 days = 800 hrs

2.   Design Walk-throughs
        100 unit/0.5 hr per unit × 2 people = 100 hrs

3.   Review the design
        100 units/1 hr per unit × 4 people = 400 hrs

4.   Redesign based on review
        20 units × 4 hrs per unit = 80 hrs

5.   Re-review the design
        20 units × 1 hrs per unit × 3 people = 60 hrs

6.   Design documentation

        150 pgs. × 2 hrs per page = 300 hrs

        Traceability matrix = 60 hrs

7.   Meetings with marketing/user/subcontractor = 100 hrs

8.   Prepare and present top-level design review = 180 hrs

Total = 2,080 hrs

e) identification of related plans, such as

— quality plan,

— configuration management plan,

— integration plan,

— test plan.

Reason: There are a number of activities required to produce a product. These activities need to be identified, costed, and scheduled. In addition, the interaction and interdependency of these activities with the other activities must be identified. The activities mentioned here are distinct enough that they warrant their own plans.

Means to ensure: The SPH identifies these activities as part of the engineering process. Each of these activities needs to be planned. Templates for the these plans should be used to develop the specific plan. These plans can be separate plans or part of the SDP plan. Supplier management must review and sign off on these plans. For instance, there may be one software development plan that encompasses all other plans, or the software development plan may focus on product design and coding while referencing subordinate stand-alone plans for testing, configuration control, document control, and quality assurance.

5.4.1 (conclusion)   The development plan should be updated as development progresses and each phase should be defined as in 5.4.2.1 before activities in that phase are started. It should be reviewed and approved before execution.

Comment: "Each phase" has already been defined in the SPH in a generic manner and explicitly in the SDP at the beginning of each project. At the end of each phase the SDP is reviewed and estimates are made for completing the remaining phases based upon the "actuals" of the completed phase. For instance, if the SDP was based on an original estimate of 100,000 source lines of code and at the end of the design phase the estimate is 125,000 source lines of code, then the original estimates for the coding or implementation phase as well must be adjusted.

Reason: Software development is really more of a research and development effort where unforeseeable problems or changes are often encountered. The problem with most software development plans is that once they have been created, they are rarely updated to reflect the dynamic situation that they are intended to reflect. At the end of each development phase, the original estimates for the next phase should be reviewed and updated based on current information. Without accurate plans, the resources to meet the plan's goals will most likely be insufficient. When this happens, the quality of the product suffers as corners are cut in the engineering process in order to stay within the plan.

Means to ensure: Project management should require a regular weekly review of the project status as compared with the plan. The senior management should require, plan, and schedule regular monthly reviews of project status vis-à-vis the plan.

The plan should be based on some quantifiable metric like number of modules to design, code, test, and integrate. Quantifiable numbers reflecting the current amount of work completed should be presented at these meetings and compared with the plan. In addition, when reporting to senior management the project management should identify the status of external dependencies over which they have no immediate control and any risks that exist to the project's schedule or budget.

5.4.2 Development Plan

5.4.2.1 Phases

The development plan should define a disciplined process or methodology for transforming the purchaser's requirements specification into a software product. This may involve dividing the work into phases, and the identification of . . .

Comment: The development plan is meant to show the resources and schedule for activities needed to develop the product based on a defined engineering process. An engineering organization need not define a process or methodology for every project. Rather, it should tailor a standard process definition in order to achieve the project's technical, budget, and schedule goals. In other words, the software development plan used to manage the project is based upon the generic engineering process defined in the SPH.

a) development phases to be carried out;

Reason: An engineering process is divided into steps or phases. The products of each phase support the succeeding phase. Having clearly defined phases allows for accurate costing, scheduling, and statusing. Defined phases also allow for reviews at the completion each phase. These reviews allow for quality checks to be performed on a phase's output and estimates concerning the following phases to be made.

Means to ensure: The development phases are defined in the SPH. The SDP should be based upon the SPH but tailored or restated for the specific project. Senior management should review the SDP to check that the plan is based upon the development phases as described in the SPH and that the resources estimated to carry out those phases are reasonable.

b) required inputs for each phase;

Reason: An engineering phase requires inputs in order for the activities within that phase to be performed.

Means to ensure: The required inputs are those identified in the SPH and defined in the SDP as tailored for the project.

c) required outputs from each phase;

Reason: An engineering phase creates outputs for use in the next phase.

Means to ensure: The required outputs are those identified in the SPH and defined in the SDP as tailored for the project.

d) verification procedures to be carried out at each phase;

Comment: This section is concerned with verification, which, for the purposes of the guideline, includes the practices and procedures used to verify that the engineering process is being followed and the testing of the by-products of the various phases (as opposed to validation, which is the testing of the complete and integrated software product).

Reason: An engineering process exists to improve the reliability of the product and to assist in the development and delivery of a product on schedule and within budget. The engineering process needs to be verified to ensure that the practices and procedures that define an engineering process are used and are effective in meeting the goals of the process.

Means to ensure: The Quality Policy should identify the need for process verification. The SPH should identify verification activities and the records of those activities that need to be kept. An audit of the records should be performed to confirm the implementation of an organization's engineering practices and procedures. The SDP or Software Quality Assurance Plan should identify the schedule, procedures, and resources devoted to this audit effort.

e) analysis of the potential problems associated with the development phases and with the achievement of the specified requirements.

Reason: Software development is a research and development effort. Some problems can be foreseen before they occur. Other problems will arise due to technical discovery that takes place during the development effort.

Means to ensure: The Quality Policy should state that risk analysis should be a step in management of the engineering process. The SPH should state that the risks associated with the project are to be identified at the beginning of the project in a risk management plan. The SPH should have a template for this plan (see Chapter 24). During the course of the project, this plan should be reviewed along with the steps being taken to minimize risk.

The risk management plan should be updated as new risks appear and old ones fade. The SDP schedules regular review of the plan. Minutes of these meetings must be kept. Attendees at this meeting should be the project manager, project technical leads, organizational level management, and, in some cases, representatives from the purchaser, if they have a part in managing the risk.

5.4.2.2 Management

The development plan should define how the project is to be managed, including the identification of . . .

Comment: A plan is more than just deliverables, dates, and subordinate plans. It must also include how the project is to be managed. Management includes statusing and action based on status. The development plan should identify the reviews that will take place, change control procedures, and methods for obtaining and reporting status.

a) schedule of development, implementation and associated deliveries;

Reason: Deliverables are needed for one phase of product development to commence and/or one organization involved in the development of a product to begin work. Therefore, schedules for these deliverables should be identified. Once the schedules are identified, the resources required to create the deliverables within the schedule time frame can be identified.

Means to ensure: The SDP is based on a product's requirements and the defined engineering process. As the guideline points out, special care should be taken to identify the external dependencies, for two reasons. First, external dependencies may be beyond the control of the project management. Second, failure in external dependencies, either in quality or timeliness of delivery, often have a major impact on a project's budget and schedule. These dependencies should be made visible to senior management and their status reported to senior management, which must deal with failures in external dependencies.

b) progress control;

Reason: No project will run by itself merely because there is a plan in place. When there is a failure to status the development effort against the SDP, an organization loses control and cannot make the changes in resource allocations, or the engineering process itself needed to deliver a product that meets requirements within schedule.

Means to ensure: The SPH should identify the means by which the engineering process is controlled. This control is based upon accurate status and review of the work being performed. The SPH should identify the project reviews and at what stages they take place, and what is to be statused and by whom on a regular (weekly, monthly) basis. The SDP identifies the schedule for these activities and their implementation. Supplier management must ensure these activities take place and take part in the review and status process.

c) organizational responsibilities, resources and work assignment;

Reason: This is a repeat of 5.4.1 (b). The intent is to make sure all staff members within the supplier organization involved in the project are aware of what is expected of them.

Means to ensure: The SPH identifies the roles and responsibilities of the various organizations responsible for developing or maintaining a software product. The SDP should be based upon the SPH and explicitly state the implementation of the engineering process. The SDP and subordinate plans should be signed off by the managers of the various organizations who are responsible for implementing the plan(s).

d) organizational and technical interfaces between different groups.

Reason: Many groups understand their own roles and responsibilities, but they may have little understanding of responsibilities of other groups or the interfaces between the various organizations responsible for developing a product. This is especially important when different groups are responsible for creating the inputs for another group's task or activity.

Means to ensure: The SPH should identify the technical exchanges (e.g., deliverables, reviews, meetings) between the various groups that should take place. The SDP must budget and schedule these activities. The SPH must be tailored for the project, and it must be read and understood by all project participants. Senior management must assume the responsibility to ensure that this cross-organizational understanding and commitment exists.

5.4.2.3   Development Methods and Tools

The development plan should identify methods for ensuring that all activities are carried out correctly. This may include . . .

Comment: The SPH identifies the activities that make up an engineering process. The SDP is meant to show the resources and time needed to create the product based on that defined process. Methodologies exist to implement the activities defined in the process and to control the various steps of implementation. If the engineering process does not spell out the specific methodologies to use (e.g., object-oriented analysis, structured analysis, boundary testing, path testing, etc.) in implementing an activity, then the development plan must do so. Much of what follows in this section could be defined in the SPH. If need be, the SPH can be tailored for individual projects.

Further comment: "Methods for ensuring that all activities are carried out correctly" could very easily refer to reviews, audits, and tests in addition to what the guideline suggests in the next three sections.

a) rules, practices and conventions for development;

Reason: Engineering organizations, by definition, have agreed-upon rules, practices, and conventions. These exist not to limit an engineer's creativity, but rather to ensure that there are no unnecessary differences, and that "best of kind" practices are used uniformly to enhance the engineer's productivity in the development of an engineered product.

Means to ensure: The SPH should define the process steps used to develop software, as well as the programming standards, design standards, and the specifications that support the process. Project management should tailor the SPH for a specific project, and senior management should approve or disapprove this tailoring based upon the tailoring's impact on quality, budget, and schedule.

b) tools and techniques for development;

Reason: An organization may make use of CASE (computer aided software engineering) tools or methodologies in analysis, design, implementation, and testing. Their planned use will affect the project's costs and schedules. Project participants should be certified as competent in their use, either through training or prior use of the specified CASE tools or techniques.

Means to ensure: The SDP should identify CASE tools, if used, and methodologies and techniques for use in development. The actual description of these tools and techniques should be referenced by the SDP. The project training plan should identify the training requirements for using the tools and techniques (see section 6.9).

c) configuration management.

Reason: Configuration management refers to the practices and procedures used to manage the product and project baselines. Changes to baselines impact budgets and schedules; therefore, such changes need to be controlled.

Means to ensure: The SDP should include, as a subordinate plan, a configuration management plan. This plan should be based upon the organization's documented configuration management process as described in the SPH (see section 6.1, Configuration Management).

5.4.3 Progress Control

Progress reviews should be planned, held and documented to ensure that outstanding resource issues are resolved and to ensure effective execution of development plans.

Comment: This is a repeat of 5.4.2.2 (b). For many software projects, senior management uses only major milestones as check points to determine the progress of a project. Senior management rarely has quantifiable means to determine the status of a project.

Reason: Senior management must be made aware of the status of projects so as to adjust the resources or schedule required to meet the projects goals. They must also be made aware of any outside influences (e.g., status of external interfaces, purchaser-supplied products or facilities, organizational turnover) that affect the project's budget and schedule or the quality of the product.

Means to ensure: The Quality Policy should call for regular reviews of the project's status. The SPH should identify these reviews as part of the engineering process. The SDP should identify these reviews as specific tasks as well as what will be statused. At these organizational-level reviews, the senior management should review a project's progress (modules designed, test cases written, lines of code written and tested, modules integrated, etc.), quality measurements (customer assigned action items, bug reports, test case failures), and risks to the project (status of external deliveries, technical constraints exceeded, rate of employee turnover) to ensure that the projects budget, schedule, and technical and quality goals are being reached.

5.4.4 Input to Development Phases

The required input to each development phase should be defined and documented. Each requirement should be defined so that its achievement can be verified. Incomplete, ambiguous or conflicting requirements should be resolved with those responsible for drawing up the requirements.

Comment: This section is a repeat of 5.4.2.1 (b). This section speaks of two topics. The first sentence speaks of inputs to each phase and the need for those inputs to be defined and documented. The remaining sentences speak to functional and performance requirements and the need to state these requirements in such a way that they can be tested.

Reasons: Software development is an engineering process with defined steps. The speed at which an engineering step is accomplished and the quality of its outputs are, to a large extent, based on the quality of the inputs to that step. Therefore a step's inputs need to be defined and checked for completeness and accuracy before the task begins.

In addition, the functional and performance requirements must be stated in such a manner that they can be tested. If, as stated, they cannot be tested, they should be identified as nontestable and be restated so they can be tested or, barring restatement, they must be deleted as a requirement.

Means to ensure: The SPH should define a generic development process, identify the inputs for each step, and contain a template for those engineering documents (e.g., requirement specifications, plans, design documents, test cases) that serve as inputs and outputs for several of the steps that make up the process. The SPH should also identify the reviews and tests that need to be performed on the products and by-products created by the engineering process. The SDP is based upon the SPH. Whereas the SPH defines the engineering process and the inputs and outputs of that process's steps in a generic manner, the SDP explicitly identifies the inputs and outputs to each engineering step and identifies the budget and schedule the activities required to produce and test these inputs and outputs.

5.4.5   Output from Development Phases

The required output from each development phase should be defined and documented. The output from each development phase should be verified and should . . .

Comment: This section is very much like the previous section, except that the reference to functional and performance requirements has been dropped. The reader will excuse us if we, like the guideline, repeat ourselves.

a) meet the relevant requirements;

Reason: The outputs of one step in the development cycle are the inputs for next step. There is a negative impact on either the next or succeeding step's budget, schedule, and, quite possibly, the quality of that step's outputs if the output of a previous step fails to meet the next step's input requirements. If an output is found deficient, a business decision must be made whether to move ahead and use the output as is and assume the risk to the next step's quality, or rework the product and assume the risk to schedule and budget.

Means to ensure: The Quality Policy should state that reviews or tests are required of all outputs of each engineering step or task to ensure that the output meets its requirements. The SPH should identify the reviews and their purpose. The SDP should identify the budget and schedule for the reviews.

b) contain or reference acceptance criteria for forwarding to subsequent phases;

Reason: Software development and maintenance is an integrated process where the products of one phase support the activities in the following phase. The time it takes to complete one phase and the quality of that phase's output depends, to a large degree, on the quality of inputs to that phase. Acceptance (or exit) criteria for entry into the next phase (or from one phase) should be defined and used to determine whether that following phase or step can begin.

Means to ensure: The SPH should specify that reviews or tests should take place at the end of each phase, step, or task. The SPH should identify a generic corrective action process for nonconforming items as well as guidelines and the quality goals for the output of each phase. The SDP should explicitly restate the generic processes and guidelines found in the SPH and identify the budgets and schedules required for their implementation.

c) conform to appropriate development practices and conventions, whether or not these have been stated in the input information;

Reason: This statement is meant to say that once engineering steps and their inputs and outputs are identified, an organization should ensure that the activities that turn inputs into outputs conform to an organization's commonly accepted methods, techniques, and conventions.

Means to ensure: The SPH should identify the review processes that each product should undergo. Reviews are meant to ensure that the product has been developed according to commonly accepted methods, techniques, and conventions as well as the correctness and completeness of the product being reviewed. The Quality Policy should state that there will be audits performed to ensure the use of "appropriate development practices and conventions." The Software Quality Assurance Plan should identify the audit activities for the project and the budget to implement those activities.

d) identify those characteristics of the product that are crucial to its safe and proper functioning;

Reason: Certain requirements, items, or modules may be crucial to the proper functioning of the product. These requirements, items, or modules should be identified so as to ensure that they receive special attention during the specification, design, implementation, and testing of both the original development effort and any enhancement activities.

Means to ensure: The SPH should state that for each phase of development a conscious effort should be made to identify and track the key requirements, items, and modules.

e) conform to applicable regulatory requirements.

Reason: A product may be required to be developed according to industry regulations and standards such as those found in government or government-regulated industries.

Means to ensure: The SDP should state that the project is being developed according to whatever industry standard applies. Reviews and audits should be performed to ensure that the product and the process conform to the applicable regulatory standard.

5.4.6 Verification of Each Phase

The supplier should draw up a plan for verification of all development phase outputs at the end of each phase.

Development verification should establish that development phase outputs meet the corresponding input requirements by means of development control measures such as . . .

Reason: A software product is developed as it passes through various phases and several steps within each phase. The quality of one step's outputs impact the next step's schedule and outputs. To ensure that the one step's output supports, rather than detracts from, the effort and quality of the next step, a check of the output should be performed before the succeeding step begins.

Means to ensure: The Quality Policy should state that verification shall take place at the end of each development phase and each step within the phase. In the SPH, identify the inputs and outputs for each phase and step. The SPH should also identify the procedures used to verify the output's correctness through reviews and tests. These verification activities and the schedule and resources required to perform them should be identified in the SDP.

a) holding development reviews at appropriate points in the development phases;

Reason: At the end of each phase, a "snapshot" of the project can be taken to ensure that the development is on track. Development reviews are held to ensure that the development phase just ending has succeeded and that inputs for the next phase or step have met their quality goals. In addition, the review ensures that the plans needed for the next phase are in place and are accurate. For instance, snapshots can be taken at the end of the requirement analysis, design, coding, and testing phases. These types of reviews should be attended by project and senior management.

Means to ensure: The Quality Policy should state that project management and possibly senior management reviews are required during and at the end of each phase of the project. The SPH should identify what reviews take place, the purpose of the review, what will be reviewed, and how action items will be managed. The SDP explicitly defines the review process and the schedule and resources required for these reviews.

b) comparing a new design with a proven similar design, if available;

Reason: Many organizations fail to take advantage of lessons learned from previous projects or the experience of senior engineers who are not directly assigned to the project. Senior engineers from other projects should review the project user interface, key algorithms, internal product design, and test cases to determine whether previous designs or implementations could be used to advantage on the current project.

Means to ensure: The Quality Policy should state that a product's design should be compared to similar products. The SPH should identify this comparison as one of the procedures within the design phase. The SDP should identify the designs that will be used for comparison as well as costs and schedule for the comparison effort.

The SPH should require than an organization maintain a repository of project designs and "lesson learned" or postmortems from previous projects. Without such a repository an organization will have difficulty in comparing designs between projects.

c) undertaking tests and demonstrations.

The verification results and any further actions required to ensure that the specified requirements are met should be recorded and checked when the

actions are completed. Only verified development outputs should be submitted to configuration management and accepted for subsequent use.

Reason: A component that has not been tested, or reviewed, and is submitted for configuration management is more likely to fail than a product that has been tested. The cost of modifying a component once it has been put under configuration control is much higher than modifying a component that has not been brought under configuration control. Additionally, the cost of modifying a component in use by a customer is much higher that modifying a component still under control of the development organization. The bottom line? Test your products before you or anyone else uses them.

There are other products of the engineering process besides software components, such as specifications, test cases, and test results. These too should be reviewed for correctness and completeness before being submitted for configuration control.

Means to ensure: In the SPH, state that no software component, or any other product component, be brought under configuration control that has not been tested or reviewed. Audits of this testing should be performed to ensure that it has taken place. The results of all levels of testing (from unit to acceptance tests) should be considered for configuration control. The SPH should generically identify the other products of the engineering process and the reviews that they should undergo before being brought under configuration control while the SDP explicitly identifies those products for a specific project.

5.5   Quality Planning

There are activities used to verify or validate the quality of a development effort's products or by-products. This section suggests that plans be defined to ensure that these activities take place. The plans for these activities can be a separate plan (a quality plan) or incorporated in other plans like the development plan, test plan, and configuration management plan.

To a large degree this section is redundant in that it repeats or overlaps subjects found in other sections of the guideline. Examples of this repetition are

> defining inputs and outputs for each development phase;

> identifying the types of test to be carried out;

> identifying the resources, schedules, and roles and responsibilities for carrying out the tests;

> configuration management; and

> defect control and corrective action.

In addition, having a separate plan to identify the resources and schedules needed to implement the quality activities (actually they are standard engineering activities) identified in this section is contrary to the goal of having these activities integrated into the engineering process and procedures used to create a quality product.

What the guideline should be addressing in this section is the need for a separate Software Quality Assurance Plan that identifies the audit process for independently assuring the use of the organization's defined process and procedures. In addition this plan should identify the plans for quality records and quality measurement (see sections 6.3 and 6.4).

11

Design and Implementation

Design is the technical kernel of a software product and to a great degree dictates the quality of the product. The quality of a product's design impacts the usability, testability, and the costs of maintaining and enhancing the product throughout its lifetime. The guideline suggests the design effort and the product itself would benefit from careful consideration of design methodologies, design rules and guidelines, internal design (not seen by the user), and a comparison of the product to designs used for previous products. Design and code reviews are an important part of the software engineering process. They should be planned and executed with the outcome of the reviews becoming part of the project documentation.

Again we point out that the guideline does not discuss the detailed software requirements analysis phase that normally precedes the design phase in the software engineering process. Rather, the guideline moves from the specification of the purchaser's requirements directly to the design and implementation phases. We view this as an unfortunate omission.

5.6 Design and Implementation

5.6.1 General

The design and implementation activities are those which transform the purchaser's requirements specification into a software product. Because of the complexity of software products, it is imperative that these activities be carried out in a disciplined manner, in order to produce a product according to specification rather than depending on the test and validation activities for assurance of quality.

Comment: Testing a product to find and fix design errors is far more costly, and less effective, than creating a solid, well-engineered design in the first place. In addition, maintaining a poorly designed product can be an expensive nightmare that drains an organization's engineering resources away from new development projects. There are well-known design methodologies (e.g., structured design, object oriented design, database normalization, error handling design, user interface design) and activities (e.g, walk-throughs, inspections, prototyping, configuration management, usability testing) that are meant to ensure the final product's quality, completeness, and correctness.

NOTE 6   The level of information disclosure to be provided to the purchaser needs to be mutually agreed to by the parties, as design and implementation processes are frequently proprietary to the supplier.

Comment: There is a fine line between the exchange of information concerning the supplier's capabilities and the status of the work being performed and, on the other hand, that which constitutes an unwarranted intrusion into the details of how the supplier performs work or the inner workings or design of the product. The supplier and purchaser must agree in the contract as to what is considered the supplier's proprietary information.

5.6.2 Design

In addition to the requirements common to all the development phases, the following aspects inherent to the design activities should be taken into account.

Comment: We are uncomfortable with the preceding statement. For example, "In addition to the requirements common to all development phases" and the word "inherent" are very open ended, and subject to interpretation. An organization should explicitly state what the requirements are for each of the development phases in the SPH and tailoring the SPH for specific projects.

a) Identification of design considerations: in addition to the input and output specifications, aspects such as design rules and internal interface definitions should be examined.

Reason: There are external design attributes that are visible to the user such as the user interface and there are internal design attributes that are invisible to the user (e.g., architecture, database, client server). Many software engineers lack an understanding of software design and design issues that will affect the reliability and maintainability of a product. There are design heuristics that can serve as guidelines for product design that, when followed, increase the likelihood of a well-engineered design. The basis of engineering is design and to assume that a development team will "naturally" do a good job of design is a mistake.

Means to ensure: State the design guidelines in the SPH, or reference these guidelines if they are in a separate document. For instance, there should be design guidelines for the system and program design, user-interface design, database design, module design, and error-handling design. During the product development phases reviews should take place to ensure that the guidelines, or approved tailorings of the guidelines, are being followed.

b) Design methodology: a systematic design methodology appropriate to the type of software product being developed should be used.

Comment: Note the phrase "appropriate to the type of software being developed." No one methodology is applicable in all cases. An engineering organization should give serious consideration as to which methodology is appropriate for a given development project.

Reason: On medium- to large-scale projects, the number of design engineers involved require a consistent design so that the product will appear to the purchaser as one whole, integrated, and consistent product.

Means to ensure: Specify in the SDP the design methodologies to be used in the design of the product and the reason why the methodology was chosen. Examples of these methodologies are object oriented design and functional decomposition. Methodologies could also apply to test case design and the types of reviews that will be held and the manner in which they are conducted.

c) Use of past design experiences: utilizing lessons learned from past design experiences, the supplier should avoid recurrences of the same or similar problems.

Reason: Take advantage of lessons learned from one project and apply that knowledge to similar projects. Failure to do this may extend the development phase as you "reinvent the wheel" or worse, you solve similar problems or bugs over and over again.

Means to ensure: In the SPH, state that the design should be reviewed by senior engineers from other projects. In the SDP, plan for the reviews and budget the hours for members of other projects to prepare and attend key reviews.

d) Subsequent processes: the product should be designed to the extent practical to facilitate testing, maintenance and use.

Reason: No engineer consciously sets out to design and develop software that is difficult to test, maintain, or use. Products with these negative attributes are developed when the user's requirements for testing a product or the operational use of the product are not understood by the development organization. Testability, usability, and maintainability requirements are just as important as the product's functional requirements since a product may be rejected by the purchaser if it cannot be tested or used in the operational environment.

Means to ensure: The Quality Policy should state that product development is based on an engineering process. The SPH identifies the various activities and reviews that take place to ensure that products being developed are testable, maintainable, and usable. The SDP should explicitly identify the methodologies and activities that are meant to ensure the creation of a testable, maintainable, and usable product and identify the budgets and schedules required to implement the engineering process in order to meet these sometimes unstated purchaser requirements.

5.6.3   Implementation

Introduction: The guideline is very light in its suggested guidelines in some sections and this section is one of them. The guideline suggests that the supplier establish and use standards for mundane subjects such as naming conventions, coding, and commentary.

In addition to the requirements common to all the development activities, the following aspects should be considered in each implementation activity.

Comment: Again, as in 5.6.2, we are uncomfortable with the guideline's wording "in addition to the requirements common to all development activities." This is an open statement, which could be interpreted in a number of different ways.

a) Rules: rules such as programming rules, programming languages, consistent naming conventions, coding and adequate commentary rules should be specified and observed.

Reason: A product, once developed, is maintained over a number of years. In many instances, the developer is not the maintainer. To minimize the effort required to maintain a product, the source code should be clear, concise, and easy to read through the consistent application of programming rules, naming conventions, and comments.

Means to ensure: An organization should have documented programming standards, not to exceed five to ten pages in length. Standards longer than 10 pages will be difficult for the developer to remember and apply, as well as audit. Using automated tools to format the source code, check for memory leaks, and calculate module complexity is recommended. The SPH should identify the coding standards and require their use on all development and maintenance projects. The SDP should reference the coding standard to be used on the project. During reviews, a conscious effort is made to determine whether the product conforms to the standard.

b) Implementation methodologies: the supplier should use appropriate implementation methods and tools to satisfy purchaser requirements.

Reason: Many times projects are started without forethought given to the methods and tools that are to be used during the development effort. Failure to identify the methods and tools and train engineers in their use impedes the development effort and most likely will have a negative effect upon schedule, budget, and possibly quality.

Means to ensure: The SDP should identify the methods and tools to be used on a project and, in the training plan, the budget and schedule required to train the engineers in their use.

5.6.4   Reviews

The supplier should carry out reviews to ensure that the requirements are met and the above methods are correctly carried out. The design or implementation

process should not proceed until the consequences of all known deficiencies are satisfactorily resolved or the risk of proceeding otherwise is known.

The section addresses the need for design reviews to ensure that the purchaser's requirements are fulfilled by the design. Reviews and audits are also meant to ensure that the methodologies and rules that were meant to be used during design were in fact used.

Comment: Many engineers consider reviews a waste of valuable time. These engineers are partially correct. Poorly run reviews, of which there are many, waste valuable time but well-run reviews add value to the engineering effort. The problems with reviews are caused by the manner in which they are prepared for and executed.

Reason: A product is created to meet requirements. An engineering organization uses commonly accepted methods to increase the likelihood of meeting requirements. One such method is reviews. At each step of the development effort there should be a check, in the form of a review, to ensure that the methods are being used and used properly, and that the step has accomplished what it was meant to accomplish.

During these reviews, problems with the product being reviewed are to be identified. After some degree of analysis, a conscious business decision can be made to continue on with the project with the identified problem still in existence or halt further progress until the problem has been eliminated.

Means to ensure: The Quality Policy should state that multilevel reviews should take place during product development. In the SPH, identify the types of required reviews, for example, marketing requirements review, contract review, user document review, software requirements document review, software development plan review, software test plan, design reviews, and code reviews. Even within these categories of reviews there are different methods to perform the reviews ranging from walk-throughs to inspections and from very formal to very informal reviews. In the SDP, plan for the reviews, and budget resources to prepare and carry out the reviews. Records of all such reviews should be under document control.

12
Testing and Validation

Testing is a complex engineering effort and must be well planned in order to be executed properly. In order to test a product the supplier must be able to identify the various levels of testing to be performed and the requirements for those levels of testing. This chapter focuses mainly on the supplier's responsibilities for testing the product from the unit tests through system-level testing and on into field tests. Generally speaking, for each level of testing the supplier must identify the requirements being tested, test methods to be used, software and hardware resources required to execute the tests, and schedule and budget required to develop the test cases, identify the expected results, and actually run the tests.

Tests should be executed in an engineering manner and the results of the tests must be analyzed to determine where product and process improvements should be made. The tests results should be saved so they can be used at a later date to validate future tests and to prove, if need be, that the product was actually tested.

5.7   Testing and Validation

5.7.1   General

Testing may be required at several levels from the individual software item to the complete software product. There are several different approaches to testing and integration.

Comment: The guideline is stating that multilevel testing is a commonly accepted principle in software engineering and that various methodologies for testing are used at different levels of testing.

Reason: Testing activities should be conducted at various phases of the system development life cycle to aid in the development of a reliable product that meets purchaser requirements within time and budget constraints. Different categories of product problems (bugs) are tested for at various levels of product development, where they would be most easy to detect and least costly to fix.

Means to ensure: The Quality Policy should state the need for multilevel testing. The SPH identifies the types of tests required for each development phase and the SDP (or a subordinate test plan) identifies and schedules the resources required to design and execute the various test cases.

In some instances, validation, field testing and acceptance testing may be one and the same activity.

Reason: The purchaser may determine that system-level testing, on a complete product, executed by the developer at the supplier or purchaser facilities, may be sufficient for the purchaser to accept ownership of the product.

If the testing is performed at the purchaser's site then there must be a process to ensure that all the patches and fixes installed during the testing are applied to a baseline copy of the product. At the conclusion of testing, a new baseline copy should be delivered and retested before the purchaser takes ownership of the product.

Means to ensure: The contract should identify the level of testing the purchaser considers sufficient before accepting the product. The contract should state that the tests results are to be delivered to the purchaser for review and approval before the purchaser accepts the product.

The document that describes the test plan may be an independent document or a part of another document, or may be composed of several documents.

Reason: Testing is a difficult and time-consuming process that needs to be planned and have personnel trained and ready to design and execute the tests. Testing and test preparation takes place during the entire product-development cycle. For instance:

Requirement phase:

> Develop preliminary test plan
>
> Identify tests cases
>
> Prepare test traceability matrix

Design phase:

> Develop test cases
>
> Update test plan

Code phase:

> Populate functional and system-level test cases
>
> Execute unit-level test case

Test phase:

> Conduct functional, integration, and system tests
>
> Conduct alpha, beta/field tests
>
> Perform regression testing as needed.

The point we, and the guideline, are trying to make is that an effort of this size needs to be planned and budgeted in order to be effective. Depending on the size and complexity of the product being developed, the test plan can be a stand-alone document or part of the SDP. For ease of maintenance and review we recommend that the test plan be a separate document.

5.7.2 Test Planning

Introduction: There are various levels of testing that can be performed on a software product. There needs to be plans in place to support this process. The plans should address

> types of testing
>
> test cases
>
> test environment
>
> resources and schedule required to create the tests
>
> resources and schedule required to execute the tests
>
> entry and exit criteria for each phase of testing
>
> external dependencies
>
> test tools
>
> technical, budget, and schedule risks.

The supplier should establish and review the test plans, specifications and procedures before starting testing activities. Considerations should be given to

a) plans for software item, integration, system test and acceptance test;

Comment: Just so there is no confusion, the purchaser is responsible for the acceptance test plan; the supplier should require the purchaser to deliver the acceptance test plan to the supplier for review. Both the purchaser and the supplier must agree as to the validity of the acceptance test plan.

Reason: Testing takes place at different product levels and at different phases during the development cycle. The types of testing and the resources required to perform the testing need to be identified and planned in order to allow the orderly (engineered) creation and execution of the test cases. Just as a product's design is reviewed, test plans and procedures need to be reviewed to ensure their correctness and completeness.

Means to ensure: The SPH should require the development of a test plan that includes identification of the various levels of testing as well as a schedule and resources required to support the development and execution of the test. This plan should be reviewed and approved by project management and possibly senior management. The purchaser may also require review of the test plans, test cases, and test results.

b) test cases, test data and expected results;

Reason: Far too often, testing is performed in an ad hoc and nonengineered manner. To ensure that all requirements have been tested for and all functions or objects work as designed, test cases have to be created that explicitly test for requirements and component functionality. Each test case must identify its test data, test procedures (how to actually run the tests), and expected test results. After the test is run, the expected results are compared to the actual results to determine whether the product being tested has passed the tests.

Means to ensure: Use a test traceablitity matrix to ensure that all requirements and functions have a test case. The matrix traces each requirement, or several requirements, to a test case. We find it quite unbelievable that so many engineering organizations lack, in some manner, this traceability capability.

For each test case, identify the following:

test case number and name

name and version number of the product or component being tested

test environment

location of test data

test procedures (or script)

expected results

actual results

test report.

c) types of test to be performed, e.g. functional tests, boundary tests, performance tests, usability tests;

Reason: At each level of testing, there are different types of testing that look for different types of errors or are meant to prove that the product works at various levels of integration: at the unit level, branch and path testing; at the component level, tests check for correct functionality; system-level tests check for product conformance to functional and technical (e.g., throughput, reliability, usability, security) requirements; usability tests (used to prove fitness for use in an operational mode) require coordination with the purchaser.

Means to ensure: The SPH identifies the various levels of testing performed in the engineering process. The test plan, as a subordinate plan to the SDP, identifies the budget and schedule required to implement the various levels of testing along with the test cases to be used.

d) test environment, tools and test software;

Reason: Testing a software product may require a separate test environment, with its own hardware and software under control of the test, versus development, organization. In many cases, the costs for a separate test environment, test tools, and test software are not factored into the overall costs of developing a product. The test environment (both hardware and software) should be created and exercised before formal testing of the product begins in order to assure its readiness.

Means to ensure: The SPH should require a test plan. The test plan should identify the hardware and software that needs to be purchased or developed in order to test the product. The test plan should identify the schedules for the delivery of the purchased products and the development of the test software. There should be management review of the test plan and the status of the plan's implementation.

The project manager should ensure that the environment needed for the product to operate has been identified, put in place, and exercised in preparation for performing the tests. This preparation should be identified as a distinct effort in the test plan or SDP.

e) the criteria on which the completion of the test will be judged;

Reason: Before running a test the expected results of the tests should be identified. Comparing expected results to actual results serves as the means by which a test can be judged successful. Additionally, other criteria may be used to determine whether a test has been completed, for instance, line of code coverage or the number of critical, major, and minor errors found.

Means to ensure: Each test case should have its expected results documented. The expected results, as well as the inputs and test procedures for running the tests, should be reviewed to ensure accuracy before the test is run and compared after the tests have been run. Test cases, procedures, expected results, and actual results should be brought under configuration control.

f) user documentation;

Reason: User documentation should describe how the product is installed and used as well as any work-arounds for known bugs in the product. Test cases should be created to ensure that this documentation is accurate and complete.

Means to ensure: The SPH should identify the need for testing user documentation as part of the overall test plan in order to ensure the accuracy and completeness of the documentation. The test plan should schedule the resources required to create the test cases based on the user documentation and to execute the test cases. The expected results on the test cases should be based upon the user documentation.

g) personnel required and associated training requirements.

Reason: To implement a plan requires people. In addition, the people have to be trained to carry out the work identified in the plan. Too often, engineers are assigned to perform the tasks that they are not fully capable of performing, and the training costs for these people are not considered in the overall costs of the project.

Means to ensure: Identify the number of people needed to perform the tasks identified in the test plan and the type of training required to execute the tasks either in the test plan or the training plan. Base the estimates on historic data or number of resources used for similar projects and the experience of the personnel available. Gaps in the background of the people assigned to do the testing can be identified and a training program put in place to prepare these engineers for testing the product.

5.7.3 Testing

Introduction: This section identifies general practices that should be followed in the testing of software products. The guideline suggests that test results should be recorded and used in order to identify problems with the product and areas where tests need to be rerun, and to determine the adequacy of the test process.

Special attention should be paid to the following aspects of testing:

Comment: This section identifies engineering practices that should be followed at all levels of testing from the unit level all the way to acceptance tests.

a) the test results should be recorded as defined in the relevant specification;

Reason: Test results should be kept as part of the permanent documentation associated with the product for a number of reasons. Results are checked to ensure that they meet the expected results, used to prove to the purchaser that tests actually were run, and used as a benchmark for comparison to the results of further tests run after changes have been made to the product.

Means to ensure: State in the SPH that test results are to be kept under configuration control. In the test plan identify the location (e.g., directories, file cabinets) where the test results are stored or refer to a section in the configuration management plan that identifies the locations.

b) any discovered problems and their possible impacts to any other parts of the software should be noted and those responsible notified so the problems can be tracked until they are solved;

Reason: Problems identified during testing are reported so that they can be addressed and resolved. In addition, a problem found in one component of the product may have an impact on other components and may cause those components to be reworked; consequently, there may be a need to coordinate the activities of a number of engineers during the problem resolution effort or the retesting that follows the implementation of a solution.

Means to ensure: The SPH should identify the problem reporting and tracking process. This process should be supported by a standard form or tool to document problems found during product testing. The SDP should identify the resources required to implement the process identified in the SPH, and the configuration management plan, or possibly the test plan, should define the details of its implementation. This process should include a regularly scheduled review of all test results. This review should be attended by representatives from testing, development, and documentation to ensure agreement concerning the problem and the solution.

c) areas impacted by any modifications should be identified and retested;

Reason: Any change to a component requires that component to be tested to ensure that the change has correctly modified the component and has not caused a different error to be introduced into that component. Additionally, this modified component should be retested with other components of the product that are related. This type of testing is generally referred to as regression testing, where the scope of testing expands beyond the component(s) that were changed to include other components that are directly and indirectly integrated with the components that have been modified.

Means to ensure:. The SPH should state that regression testing is required whenever changes are made to any component of a product and that the testing may be expanded to other components of the product. The test plan should identify the regression test cases that describe the "suite" of components that are retested when any one of the components that make up the suite has been modified.

d) test adequacy and relevancy should be evaluated;

Reason: Just as there can be components with errors in them, there can be test cases with invalid test data, procedures, expected results, and where the scope of testing may not be adequate. Problems in the test cases, left undetected, can cause valuable project time to be spent proving that the problem lies not with the component being tested, but rather with the test case itself. In addition, customer-reported bugs are an indication not only of product failure but failure in the testing of that product. When this occurs, a review of the test cases (as well as the process used to develop the test cases) with adjustments is required.

Means to ensure: The SPH should state that test cases and test results should be reviewed and signed-off by the organizations responsible for the specification, development, documentation, and support of the product. The SDP should identify the resources required for these reviews as well as the schedule for holding the review. In addition, the SPH should require a review of test cases whenever a bug is reported from the field to determine whether the test cases need to be modified.

e) the hardware and software configuration should be considered and documented.

Reason: A software product's ability to operate in the actual hardware and software environment that it is meant to operate in must be tested. Plans must be in place to create a test suite of hardware and software at either the supplier or purchaser site that can be devoted to testing a product in an environment as close to the target environment as possible.

Means to ensure: The System Specification should explicitly identify the software and hardware environments within which the product must operate. Third-party software must be identified explicitly by name and version. Hardware components and their version numbers must also be explicitly identified. Any site-specific configuration settings that exist in the purchaser's production environment must also be identified. The supplier's software test plan and the purchaser's acceptance test plan should describe in detail the test environment, and both plans should be reviewed by the supplier and the purchaser.

5.7.4   Validation

Introduction: The guideline considers validation as the testing that is performed by the supplier on a version of the product that is intended to be delivered to the purchaser. Software testing can occur before validation but that type of testing is considered by the guideline to be verification of components of the product as opposed to validation of an entire product.

Before offering the product for delivery and purchaser acceptance, the supplier should validate its operation as a complete product, when possible under conditions similar to the application environment as specified in the contract.

Reason: The supplier needs to do a full, system-level test to ensure that the product meets the functional and technical requirements. This testing cannot be done at the component level. As mentioned before, in 5.7.3 (e), it is important to test the product in the hardware and software configuration specified in the System Specification.

Means to ensure: The SPH should identify system-level testing as one of the levels of testing to be performed. The supplier's test plan should identify the schedule, resources (both personnel and physical), and test cases to test the product as a complete and integrated system. A test traceablity matrix should be used to trace requirements to specific test cases so as to ensure completeness of the test cases. The supplier should request from the purchaser operational data files that reflect the actual use of the product. Both the supplier and the purchaser should review the test cases to ensure the adequacy of the test cases.

5.7.5   Field Testing

Introduction: Field testing takes place at a site other than the supplier's that is as close to an operational environment as possible. The guideline suggests that the field tests should be planned and that the supplier and purchaser will need to coordinate their efforts in the support of this type of testing.

Where testing under field conditions is required, the following concerns should be addressed:

Comment: Many times, it is difficult to simulate a field or actual user environment. This step is sometimes referred to as a beta test, in which the product is installed at a user site and the product is used in the operational environment, but both the purchaser and the supplier need to ensure that the beta test will not cause operational failure.

a) the features to be tested in the field environment;

Reason: Field testing should be a planned event in order to minimize the impact on the user's regular work, while maximizing the benefits of the test effort.

Means to ensure: Identify in the contract that field testing the product is a requirement. The SPH should identify this as a phase within the engineering process. This portion of the SPH is likely to be fairly general in nature due to the variability of individual contracts. A field test plan may evolve during the development phase.

The plan should identify where the field tests are to occur, the features to be tested, the test environment (hardware, software, environment settings), test cases (with inputs and expected outputs), purchaser responsibilities for supporting the field test, and a schedule along with the personnel needed to run the test cases and evaluate the test results. The plan will most likely need to be co-developed by the purchaser and supplier; consequently, the two organizations will need to develop and plan to create a field test plan. This field test plan and the plan to develop the field test plan should both be contract deliverables that need supplier and purchaser review and approval.

b) the specific responsibilities of the supplier and purchaser for carrying out and evaluating the test;

Reason: Field testing a product requires the cooperation of both the purchaser and the supplier. Both parties have responsibilities that they must meet, as well as responsibilities that they may have to share. For instance, the purchaser has to supply a site where the product can be tested, a test environment, and quite possibly personnel to run or help administer the test. Access by the supplier to the purchaser's facilities and systems may have to be allowed but still controlled by the purchaser. The supplier has to supply the product, and possibly personnel to run the test. Even more importantly, the supplier must plan to have the resources and procedures in place to provide rapid turnaround for fixes to problems reported during field testing.

Means to ensure: Identify in the contract that both the supplier and the purchaser are required to develop a plan to support field testing. The supplier's SDP should identify the resources and schedule required for developing the plan and supporting the actual field tests. A review of these plans should be a contract requirement to ensure common understanding and agreement as to the roles and responsibilities for both the purchaser and supplier concerning field testing of the product.

c) restoration of the user environment (after test).

Reason: Field testing a product may cause the purchaser's production environment and systems to be altered to support the tests. It is important to restore the purchaser's environment and system (e.g., databases, system settings, etc.) to their original state after the tests are complete so as to allow the resumption of normal operations. The purchaser should take primary responsibility for this effort with the support by the supplier.

Means to ensure: The field test plan should identify the purchaser's and supplier's responsibility for restoring all systems and environments to the pre–field test state at the end of field testing. The plan should identify what is backed up, how and where the backups are stored, the procedures to perform the restore, and the tests that are run to ensure the user environment has been restored, and the personnel who perform the restore activities.

13

Purchaser Acceptance

Acceptance testing is performed by the purchaser. The guideline points out the need for this to be a formal process planned well in advance of the actual testing. Both the supplier and the purchaser must agree on the validity of the acceptance test cases and the accuracy of the results of those test cases being executed.

An acceptance test plan should identify the schedule, resources, roles and responsibilities, test cases, and success criteria well before the actual tests are executed. Key issues that are involved in acceptance testing are product delivery, installation, and the availability of key personnel needed to deal with the installation and testing effort as well as any problems that may arise during that effort.

5.8 Acceptance

5.8.1 General

When the supplier is ready to deliver the validated product, the purchaser should judge whether or not the product is acceptable according to previously agreed criteria and in a manner specified in the contract.

The method of handling problems detected during the acceptance procedure and their disposition should be agreed between the purchaser and supplier and should be documented.

Reason: The purchaser should develop its own tests to ensure that the product being delivered meets requirements and operational use goals and not rely upon the supplier's test cases and test results. These acceptance tests should be reviewed by the supplier for correctness and both the supplier and purchaser must agree to the correctness of these tests. A process must be identified to solve problems that arise during acceptance testing that includes problem identification, tracking, and delivery of software fixes to the purchaser in order to avoid delay and confusion at this critical stage.

Means to ensure: The contract should state purchaser and supplier responsibility concerning acceptance testing. The supplier's SPH should identify acceptance testing as one of the development steps. The SPH should identify in general terms the activities that take place during acceptance testing due to the variability from one project to the next, focusing not so much on the tests themselves, since they are the responsibility of the purchaser, but rather on the support that the supplier may have to render during this phase.

If the purchaser requires the supplier to aid in acceptance testing or resolve problems that arise during this phase, the SDP should reflect this by stating the schedule and resources required to meet this responsibility. A plan to implement problem-reporting procedures and solve these problems during acceptance testing should be created, based on the process described in the SPH, and reviewed by both purchaser and supplier. The priority categories for problems should be identified and acceptable response time for the different categories should also be identified and documented in the contract.

The purchaser's acceptance criteria should be identified as a purchaser deliverable in the contract. Both the supplier and the purchaser should be aware that an evolving set of acceptance criteria, whether based on evolving requirements or on the growing understanding concerning the product on the part of the purchaser, may cause the product budget and schedule to slip. Both purchaser and supplier management should pay particular attention to this part of the overall plan and process due to the impact it can have on budget, schedule, and purchaser/supplier relationships.

5.8.2   Acceptance Test Planning

Before carrying out acceptance activities, the supplier should assist the purchaser to identify the following:

Comment: The degree of assistance the supplier renders the purchaser may vary from none to giving the purchaser direction as to schedule, procedures, environment, and acceptance criteria. In fact, everything in this section could be, and in many cases is, dictated by the purchaser with little or no role being played by the supplier.

For sake of further discussion, we assume that the supplier and the purchaser have a shared responsibility for the following, but the key point is that the supplier must ensure that the purchaser's acceptance test plan accurately tests the product and that problems discovered during acceptance testing are with the product and not with faulty acceptance tests.

a) time schedule;

Reason: Every engineering activity needs a schedule so that resources can be made available and related efforts can by synchronized. The further out in the entire process that schedules are created (and acceptance test is as far out as you can get), the less accurate the schedules will be. Therefore, both the supplier and purchaser have to work together to identify the schedule for acceptance testing and adjust the schedule as reality intrudes upon the development schedules that the acceptance schedule is based upon. The start date and duration of the acceptance test is an estimate and should be considered with a certain amount of flexibility in mind.

Means to ensure: The contract should identify the start date and duration of the acceptance test phase. This date should be based on the development schedule and the purchaser need date for a fully tested and operational product. At major project reviews validate the accuracy of the acceptance test start date based on current project status and update accordingly.

b) procedures for evaluation;

Reason: The supplier may have to work with the purchaser to ensure the purchaser has enough understanding of the product to enable the purchaser to test the product. The supplier and the purchaser need to agree that whatever procedures are designed will be a legitimate test of the product.

Means to ensure: In the contract, state that the purchaser should review the product at different stages of development so as to gain an understanding of the product, that the purchaser must have access to the supplier's test tools and test cases in order to create their own test procedures, and that the supplier must review the acceptance test cases and procedures and agree to their accuracy. The SDP should schedule time and resources to support these various reviews.

c) software/hardware environments and resources;

Reason: The acceptance test plan should identify the hardware and software environment required to test the product and the activities required to prepare that environment for testing the product. In addition, the purchaser may need the support of the supplier to configure the software product delivered by the supplier or the hardware and software environment that the product will be tested in.

Means to ensure: The contract should state that the supplier is to assist the purchaser in identifying and configuring the acceptance test environment. The purchaser should make this part of the acceptance test plan, and ensure that the plan is reviewed and agreed to by the supplier.

d) acceptance criteria.

Reason: The purchaser may have a difficult time identifying the acceptance criteria for the product. This may be due to the lack of experience on the part of the purchaser or a limited understanding of the product being delivered. The supplier can assist the purchaser in developing acceptance criteria. Assistance by the supplier, leading to a common understanding of the acceptance criteria, will minimize misunderstandings concerning whether a product has passed acceptance test.

The purchaser must be made to realize that even if the supplier assists in defining the acceptance criteria, the purchaser is responsible for the accuracy of such criteria. In addition, once schedules and budgets are developed based upon the accepted criteria, any supplier expenses caused by changing the criteria will be borne by the purchaser.

Means to ensure: The contract should state that the supplier must review acceptance criteria or assist the purchaser in developing the acceptance criteria. The acceptance criteria should be identified during the requirements definition phase or very early during the design phase. The contract should also require a review of the criteria by the supplier and purchaser and that any outstanding issues be addressed before acceptance testing begins. The budget and schedule required to support these reviews should be identified in the supplier's SDP.

5.9   Replication, Delivery and Installation

Introduction: Replication and delivery are straightforward processes that are performed after a product has been developed or enhanced and must now be sent to the purchaser. Installation, on the other hand, may require coordination between the purchaser and the supplier. The level of coordination depends upon the complexity of the product and the number of purchaser sites that use the product. Installation planning should address schedules, available personnel, site access, and acceptance testing or "bring-up" testing that is to be performed at the various sites.

5.9.1   Replication

Replication is a step which should be conducted prior to delivery. In providing for replication, consideration should be given to the following:

Comment: Replication is very much a quality assurance activity. Great care has to be taken to ensure that the correct and complete version of the product is replicated. Tremendous effort has been spent to get a product ready to ship to a purchaser. A wise manager would test the replication, delivery, and installation procedures before arriving at this stage.

a) the number of copies of each software item to be delivered;

Reason: The purchaser may require more than one copy of the product. Multiple copies drive the cost and schedule of the replication effort, especially if the replication is done by a third-party vendor.

Means to ensure: The contract should specify the number of copies to be delivered. The content of copies being shipped need to be checked before shipment to the purchaser by the supplier and upon receipt by the purchaser to ensure completeness. This same process should be followed if the supplier is contracting with a third party for the replication of the product.

b) the type of media for each software item, including format and version, in human-readable form;

Reason: The distribution media depend on the means the purchaser uses to install the product. For example, if a product is going to be distributed on CD-ROM, will the customer(s) have the capability to read CD-ROM? If the intent is to download the product (or patches to the product), will the purchaser allow on-line access by the supplier to the purchaser's system?

Means to ensure: The type of media and format used for product delivery should be identified in the contract. The product version needs to be identified so that the version delivered can be checked against the version expected. The configuration management plan should detail the product release procedures.

c) the stipulation of required documentation such as manuals and user guides;

Reason: A software product is made up of more than just the software. Operator manuals, installation guides, known problem lists, etc., can all be part of a software deliverable.

Means to ensure: The required documentation (by type and number) needs to be identified in the System Specification (contract, Statement of Work, or marketing requirements document). The documents specified need to be created, reviewed, approved, and version-controlled by the supplier. These activities should be part of the supplier's SDP and subordinate plans such as the configuration management plan and the documentation plan.

d) copyright and licensing concerns addressed and agreed to;

Reason: Questions may arise as to who owns the rights to the product and the duration of ownership. For instance, a purchaser may contract with a supplier for the development of a product that the purchaser may not want the supplier to make commercially available to the purchaser's competitors. The purchaser may also want to make copies of copyrighted material whose copyright is owned by the supplier.

Means to ensure: Copyright and license ownership need to be identified in the contract.

e) custody of master and back-up copies where applicable, including disaster recovery plans;

Reason: A great deal of effort goes into creating a product. The product's "gold" copy, or master copy, must be safeguarded to serve as a base from which to evolve the product and also to create copies of the product for additional shipments to the purchaser. The purchaser needs to identify whether they are responsible for the master and backup copies, if the supplier is responsible, or whether this is a shared responsibility.

Means to ensure: The contract should state which organization has what responsibility concerning custody of master and backup copies. If the supplier has this responsibility, then the purchaser should require that a backup/recovery plan, which specifies how the supplier safeguards the product during development and maintenance, is a contract deliverable. This plan could be part of the supplier's configuration management plan.

The supplier management should review this plan. The supplier organization, and the purchaser, if they own the rights to the product, should maintain master and backup copies in a secured area, separate from the development area.

f) the period of obligation of the supplier to supply copies.

Reason: The purchaser may require multiple releases of the same product and future versions generated by updates to the product caused by problem fixes or product enhancements.

Means to ensure: The supplier's obligation in this matter should be identified in the contract and SOW. The methods by which this obligation is fulfilled should be detailed in the supplier's maintenance plan.

5.9.2 Delivery

Provisions should be made for verifying the correctness and completeness of copies of the software product delivered.

Reason: There is a possibility that the delivered product may be the wrong version of the product or an incomplete copy of the product. Both the supplier and purchaser should work independently to ensure the correctness and completeness of the software product delivered.

Means to ensure: A version description document (much like a manufacturing bill of materials, see Chapter 24) should be created that identifies all of the product's components and their version numbers. The supplier should audit the product's components before shipping to the purchaser. Upon arrival, the purchaser should audit the product components to ensure that the product received is the version that was expected and is complete. Records of these audits should be maintained. This step should be identified in both organization's release/acceptance procedures.

5.9.3 Installation

The roles, responsibilities and obligations of the supplier and purchaser should be clearly established, taking into account the following:

Comment: A product needs to be installed at a purchaser site. The installation may require more than just mounting a tape or inserting diskettes. The installation may be a detailed effort requiring the configuration of a product for a site-specific environment, limited acceptance testing or "bring-up testing," proliferation within the purchaser's organizations, bring-up tests on proliferated systems, and rapid solutions for unexpected problems that may arise.

The purchaser should have a plan in place to manage this effort. The supplier may have to supply engineering resources to support the installation and bring-up of the product at a purchaser site. These plans should be contract deliverable from the purchaser to the supplier. The plans should reviewed by the supplier before the start of their planned activities. The chance that the supplier will be required to keep engineering resources committed to a project longer than planned is minimized if the purchaser is prepared for installing and testing of a product.

a) schedule, including out-of-normal working hours and weekends;

Reason: Installing and proliferating a product should have a minimal impact on a purchaser's normal processing. The individuals installing a product may be required to work flexible hours so as not to affect the normal processing. In addition, the engineers installing and "bringing-up" a product must work through problems as they arise and be prepared to work sometimes long and irregular hours.

Means to ensure: The contract should require an installation and proliferation plan. This plan should show, at a minimum, the schedule and resources required to prepare and installation for the product, installing the product, testing the product, and proliferating the various purchaser sites and systems. The plan should be reviewed and approved by both the purchaser and supplier.

b) access to purchaser's facilities (security badges, passwords, escorts);

Reason: The supplier's personnel may be required to help with the installation and proliferation of the product. To facilitate (and control) this effort, the purchaser must be prepared administratively to accommodate the supplier's personnel on site.

Means to ensure: The installation/proliferation plan should identify and schedule the administrative tasks required to prepare for the supplier's access to the purchaser's facilities.

c) availability of skilled personnel;

Reason: In order to expedite the installation and bring-up of a product with minimal impact on the purchaser's production and the supplier's schedules, both the purchaser and supplier should staff the effort with people with a thorough understanding of the product and the environment in which it is to operated.

Means to ensure: In the detailed installation and proliferation plan, identify key individuals preferably by name and title from both purchase and supplier organizations who must be available to support this effort. Examples of these individuals might be project and product managers, technical leads, development engineers, users, test engineers, configuration managers, and quality assurance personnel.

d) availability and access to purchaser's systems and equipment;

Reason: The supplier personnel assigned to install the system will need access to the system. In addition to facility access, access to purchaser systems via logins and passwords will most likely be necessary. If the systems that the product is to be tested on are being used in production, then the purchaser must schedule time on these systems to permit testing.

Means to ensure: The installation and proliferation plan should specify the systems that the supplier must have access to and the dates and time that supplier is allowed access. A member of the purchaser organization should be identified by name or title to ensure the supplier's access to both purchaser facilities and systems.

e) the need for validation as part of each installation should be determined contractually;

Reason: To ensure that the installation on every system is done correctly and that the product works in a production environment. This is sometimes referred to as a "bring-up test." It usually does not require a full system-level test.

Means to ensure: Plans for bring-up tests may be part of the acceptance test plan or its own separate plan. The date and location of the installations are part of the plan as well as the definition of the test cases, test data, expected results, and the resources required to test the installation. These plans need to be a contract deliverable from the purchaser to the supplier only if the supplier is required to support these activities or if the supplier must be available to respond to problems during this phase.

f) a formal procedure for approval of each installation upon completion.

Reason: There needs to be a bring-up test performed to ensure that the installation was done correctly, and that the product works in a production environment.

Means to ensure: Define tests, test procedures, and test reports to be used during installation tests. Run the tests, compare the actual output to the expected output, note deviations, and document the success or failure of the test.

14

Software Maintenance

The guideline points out that the product maintenance, or enhancement, has all the same aspects as product development. Analysis, design, implementation, and testing of changes to the product must all be planned, scheduled, and performed. An especially important issue that the guideline identifies is that the purchaser and the supplier must agree to the timing and content of product releases.

5.10 Maintenance

5.10.1 General

When maintenance of the software product is required by the purchaser, after initial delivery and installation, this should be stipulated in the contract. The supplier should establish and maintain procedures for performing maintenance activities and verifying that such activities meet the specified requirements for maintenance.

Maintenance activities for software products are typically classified into the following:

a) problem resolution;

b) interface modification;

c) functional expansion or performance improvement.

Comment: Maintenance has all of the same aspects as development of the original product. Regardless of the reason for performing the maintenance, the phases are the same: analysis, planning/resource allocation, design, implementation, test, and installation/acceptance tests.

The intent here is for the purchaser to ensure that the supplier has an engineering environment and process that will allow the supplier to implement changes in the product in an engineering manner. There is no need for a special maintenance process description; the same process used for development can and should be used for maintenance. There may be some tailoring of the SPH to prepare for its use in a maintenance program. Maintenance can include minor to major enhancements and bug fixes. For enhancement, the maintenance process should look very much like the development process. Bug fixes, while still requiring formality, should be handled with less administrative effort than required for enhancements. Special emphasis should be placed on configuration management, regression testing, and product release procedures.

The items to be maintained, and the period of time for which they should be maintained, should be specified in the contract. The following are examples of such items:

a) **program(s);**

b) **data and their structures;**

c) **specifications;**

d) **documents for purchaser and/or user;**

e) **documents for supplier's use.**

Comment: If the contract is being written before the product is fully developed, the specific items to be maintained may not be known at the time that the maintenance contract is being written. A general statement concerning the programs and data structures should suffice. Regardless of when the maintenance contract is written, if the documents are specified as deliverables, they should be specified by name at this point.

The supplier's SPH identifies the product documentation used by the supplier in development or maintenance of a product, which makes it questionable whether it has to be named in a contract, as it is for the supplier's, and not the purchaser's, use.

5.10.2 Maintenance Plan

Comment: Much of what is discussed in this section is discussed again and in more detail in section 6.1, Configuration Management.

All maintenance activities should be carried out and managed in accordance with a maintenance plan defined and agreed beforehand by the supplier and purchaser. The plan should include the following:

a) **scope of maintenance;**

Reason: To identify those components of the product that are to be maintained, so that the supplier can predict the cost for the effort and plan for resources to support the maintenance effort.

Means to ensure: The maintenance plan should identify the products that need to be maintained and develop estimates for maintaining these components. Supplier management should review and give signature approval to this plan. This plan should be a contract deliverable so that it can be reviewed by the purchaser.

b) identification of the initial status of the product;

Reason: Before maintaining or enhancing a product, its initial configuration must be established to serve as a baseline (e.g., components, status of components, etc.) for future maintenance and enhancements. Both the purchaser and supplier must agree on this baseline.

Means to ensure: A version description document should be used to identify the initial product configuration and baselines. This document should identify all components and their version, as well as the other product baselines (e.g., specifications, test cases, test results, development tools, etc.) that are to be used in the maintenance of the software product.

A list of known problems and enhancements that the purchaser wants addressed must be documented before conclusion of contract negotiation so that the supplier and the purchaser can come to an agreement concerning the costs and schedule required to update the product baseline.

c) support organization(s);

Reason: The various supplier organizations responsible for the maintenance of a product must be aware of their roles in the maintenance effort, so they can schedule and budget the resources required to support the plan.

Means to ensure: The SPH should require that each support organization reviews the purchaser's maintenance requirements and, based upon the review, each of the support organizations submits a detailed budget and schedule. These estimates form the basis of the maintenance plan.

d) maintenance activities;

Reason: The supplier organization needs to show that it has a defined engineering process for maintaining a product. The purchaser should review this defined process to be sure that such a process is in place.

Means to ensure: The supplier should reference the SPH as the definition of the organization's maintenance activities and identify any tailoring of the SPH, which makes it suitable for use in maintaining a software product, in the maintenance plan.

e) maintenance records and reports.

Reason: Changes to a product must be tracked to ensure that the product's baselines (e.g., design documents, test cases, software modules) are updated in a controlled and engineering manner. Records concerning the maintenance efforts should be produced to ensure that the changes are correct and complete. Reports should be generated to show that the maintenance efforts are on schedule and within budget.

Means to ensure: Maintenance means changes due to enhancements or bug fixes. Changes to the product and its baselines are controlled by the configuration management process discussed in more detail later (see section 6.1, Configuration Management).

5.10.3   Identification of the Initial Status of the Product

The initial status of the product to be maintained should be defined, documented and agreed to by both supplier and purchaser.

Comment: This has already been identified and discussed in 5.10.2 (b).

5.10.4   Support Organization

It may be necessary to establish an organization, with representatives from both supplier and purchaser, to support the maintenance activities.

Reason: Product support may be a long-running effort that requires dedicated resources. This is often seen in the government sector or large commercial organizations that depend upon third-party organizations to develop and maintain their systems. Dedicated resources in both the supplier and purchaser organizations to support the maintenance activities may be required to ensure the level of support required by the purchaser.

Since activities in the maintenance stage cannot always be carried out on a scheduled basis, this organization should be flexible enough to cope with the unexpected occurrence of problems.

Reason: There are four types of maintenance support: problem resolution, interface modification, functional expansion, and performance enhancement. For problem resolution, the normal help-desk and bug-fix processes that all engineering companies have to some degree should be analyzed by the purchaser to ensure that it meets the purchaser's need for timely turnaround of problems. Interface modification and functional expansion or performance improvement, in other words, enhancement requests, are very much project oriented and treated like any other purchaser request.

The supplier and the purchaser need to identify and negotiate requirements, costs, and schedules for such efforts for enhancement efforts. The purchaser should be aware that the supplier may be more interested in developing new products and seeking new business opportunities as opposed to supporting a previous purchaser's maintenance of a previously delivered product; consequently the supplier may demand a premium for maintenance support.

It may also be necessary to identify facilities and resources to be used for the maintenance activities.

Reason: The maintenance activities may be of such magnitude that dedicated physical resources are required to support the activity. Dedicated resources ensure that the purchaser requests for support will not have to compete for supplier resources against other demands.

Method to ensure: The maintenance contract should identify in detail the facilities and resources that are to be supplied by the purchaser to supplier or contracted from the supplier by the purchaser and whether these facilities and resources are to be used solely for supporting the product under contract or may be shared for the support of other products.

5.10.5   Types of Maintenance Activities

All changes to the software (for reasons of problem resolution, interface modifications, functional expansion or performance improvement) carried out during maintenance should be made in accordance with the same procedures, as far as possible, used for the development of the software product. All such changes should also be documented in accordance with the procedures for document control and configuration management.

Comment: All changes to the software should go through the same steps the software development goes through (i.e., analysis, design, code, and test). The degree to which these steps are followed will depend on the size of the change and the purchaser's need for the change (e.g., emergency fixes versus planned enhancement). The purchaser has an obvious interest in the supplier's approach, because it dictates the amount of time required to implement the changes and the quality of the updated product.

a) Problem resolution: problem resolution involves the detection, analysis and correction of software nonconformities causing operational problems. When resolving problems, temporary fixes may be used to minimize downtime and permanent modifications carried out later.

Reason: Once again the guideline points out that the maintenance process, even for problem (bug) resolution, is a step-by-step engineering process. The guideline recognizes that a certain amount of flexibility is needed to allow for temporary or "quick" fixes for problems that may be causing serious impacts to the purchaser's operations.

Means to ensure: The Quality Policy should state that maintenance activities follow an engineering process. The SPH states that the enhancement process is a tailored version of the development process. The SPH should address, possibly in a section concerning configuration management, the process for problem identification, analysis, and implementation procedures. This process should describe the supplier's policy for addressing serious, time-constrained problem resolution outside the normal enhancement and problem-resolution process by defining a expedited problem-resolution process.

b) Interface modification: interface modifications may be required when additions or changes are made to the hardware system, or components, controlled by the software.

Reason: A software product is usually part of a larger system. The other products that make up this system may change their external interfaces, which may require a change in the software product.

Means to ensure: In the maintenance contract the interfaces to other products (hardware, software) should be identified by product name and version. The contract should reference the technical documentation that describes in detail these interfaces. The contract should state that any change to the interfaces may require maintenance to be performed on the supported product with the costs to be borne by the purchaser.

c) Functional expansion or performance improvement: functional expansion or performance improvement of existing functions may be required by the purchaser in the maintenance stage.

Reason: Most products are enhanced during their life cycle. The purchaser should make sure that the supplier has a process in place to support enhancements to the product. The process for "functional expansion or performance improvement" is the same for product development, but is most likely on a smaller scale.

The question to answer here is whether the purchaser "may" require enhancements or "will" require enhancements. If the answer is "will," then the purchaser and the supplier should work out a contract to allow the supplier to plan for the resources required to make the enhancements; otherwise, the purchaser requests for enhancements will be delayed until the supplier has acquired the resources to fulfill the request.

Means to ensure: The contract should identify the level of support required of the supplier, whether for bug fixes or product enhancement, and identify the near- to mid-term enhancements planned for the product.

5.10.6   Maintenance Records and Reports

All maintenance activities should be recorded in predefined formats and retained. Rules for the submission of maintenance reports should be established and agreed upon by the supplier and purchaser.

Comment: Maintenance records and reports deal with requested and implemented changes to the product and its baselines. Communication content is high in these activities and the information needed must be complete and accurate. Both the purchaser and supplier should work together to identify the format of these records and reports as well as a process that ensures the exchange of these documents between the purchaser and supplier is handled in an efficient and business-like manner.

The maintenance records should include the following items for each software item being maintained:

a) list of requests for assistance or problem reports that have been received and the current status of each;

Reason: The supplier and purchaser need to prioritize and track the status of problem reports and enhancement requests in order to ensure that they are being processed in an expeditious manner and that the components affected by the request have been identified and are being modified and tested. The purchaser needs to have confidence in the supplier's ability to manage the problem-resolution process. The purchaser should look for the documentation that shows that the supplier has a defined engineering maintenance program.

Means to ensure: The SPH should define the management process for problem resolution. This management process is generally referred to as configuration management which is discussed in section 6.1.

b) organization responsible for responding to requests for assistance or implementing the appropriate corrective actions;

Reason: To avoid confusion and delays in resolving problems, the supplier should identify the point of contact by name and title for problem assistance and the roles and responsibilities of the various supplier organizations in the problem-resolution process.

Means to ensure: The maintenance contract should identify the supplier point of contact for requests for assistance. The SPH identifies the maintenance process and the roles and responsibilities of the various organizations in support of the maintenance activities. The maintenance plan identifies the resources required to perform the maintenance activities.

c) priorities that have been assigned to the corrective actions;

Reason: The supplier and purchaser organizations may lack a consistent understanding concerning the priority of the outstanding corrective action requests. There should be a regular review of the outstanding corrective action requests to ensure that the purchaser and supplier are in agreement as to the priorities or the change request and that the requests with the highest priority are being addressed.

Means to ensure: The SPH should identify the need for prioritizing the requests before resources are assigned to perform the corrective action. This prioritization usually takes place during a review held by the configuration control board (see section 6.1). The requirement for the purchaser and supplier to engage in joint reviews of purchaser requests for changes and for the purchaser to prioritize the requests should be stated in the maintenance contract.

d) results of the corrective actions;

Reason: The supplier should keep a record of the changes that have been made to the product in response to the corrective action request and the fact that the changes have been tested and the results reviewed and approved. A second reason for keeping accurate data concerning changes to baselines is to allow the changes to be backed out if it is discovered that the changes have caused unforeseen problems.

Means to ensure: The SPH should require recording and review of the corrective actions as part of the engineering process used to resolve problem requests. The supplier should maintain the records of the corrective actions as part of the product baseline documentation.

e) statistical data on failure occurrences and maintenance activities.

The record of the maintenance activities may be utilized for evaluation and enhancement of the software product and for improvement of the quality system itself.

Reason: There needs to be a closed-loop management process for software development efforts. The back end of this process is the problem reporting and determination of the costs for nonconforming products. Without quantifiable information, supplier management cannot make an engineering assessment as to where process improvements need to be made or what components of the product could be improved by a partial or total reengineering.

Means to ensure: The SPH should define a process that supports tracking problem reports against released versions, reviewing reports for failure analysis, and recording the costs to correct defects. Data gathered in this process form the basis for a metrics program used to improve both the engineering process and its products.

5.10.7   Release Procedures

The supplier and purchaser should agree and document procedures for incorporating changes in a software product resulting from the need to maintain performance.

Comment: "Maintain performance" is a euphemism for fixing bugs in a released product that are causing problems that severely impact the products already in use by the purchaser.

These procedures should include the following:

a) ground rules to determine where localized "patches" may be incorporated or release of a complete updated copy of the software product is necessary;

Reason: The purchaser may use the product at several locations. A problem with the product may be exhibited in only one or two locations, or the problem may only have a significant impact at one or two locations. The creation and release of "patches" is a time-consuming and administratively difficult process for the supplier organization. A balance needs to be struck between the release of the product for site-specific reasons or whether it would make more sense to release a complete, updated product for all sites.

Means to ensure: In the contract, identify the measures used to justify a patch release. An example used by one of the authors is that when a product can cause misprocessing or a decrease system throughput by 2% than the supplier must address the problem quickly and release a patch version of the product.

b) descriptions of the types (or classes) of releases depending on their frequency and/or impact on the purchaser's operations and ability to implement changes at any point in time;

Reason: This is a very important issue. The purchaser has to devote resources to implement a product release. If the releases are too frequent, the purchaser may refuse to implement the release in order to avoid the impact the implementation has on normal processing. If, for instance, the supplier is releasing an updated version of the product every eight weeks and it takes the purchaser ten weeks to test and proliferate the product, then the purchaser may begin to skip product releases. When this happens, the supplier may have to support multiple versions of a product at multiple purchaser sites.

Means to ensure: The purchaser, as the end user who the product is meant for, must direct the supplier regarding the planned release cycle for new releases.

c) methods by which the purchaser will be advised of current or planned future changes;

Comment: This is an interesting statement considering the guideline's scope, which is meant to be applied to contractual situations. This statement could be interpreted to mean that the supplier dictates when and what changes to the product will be released to the purchaser. A much stronger case could be made that since the purchaser is the user of the product, pays for its development and maintenance, and is the party most affected by a product release, that it is the purchaser who is the senior partner in any discussions concerning the timing or content of a product release.

Reason: The purchaser and the supplier must agree on the changes that will be in a product release. Otherwise, the purchaser may review the product release and determine that upgrading to the new release is not worth the effort.

Means to ensure: In the contract and the SPH, specify that the purchaser must review and approve all changes planned for a product release before the work on the product release begins. The changes that need not be reviewed and approved by the purchaser are those internal to the product itself that are not noticeable by users of the product.

d) methods to confirm that changes implemented will not introduce other problems;

Reason: A release, whether it is a patch or a major version, could cause unexpected problems with software that previously worked and was not "touched" by the changes incorporated in the patch release or the regularly scheduled release.

Means to ensure: The SPH should state that the supplier needs to run regression tests against any changes before shipping the product to the purchaser. The maintenance plan (similar to the SDP) should explicitly identify the plans and procedures for this type of testing. The purchaser should run acceptance tests whenever it receives a new product before the product is used in the purchaser's operations.

e) requirements for records indicating which changes have been implemented and at what locations, for multiple products and sites.

Reason: A software product may be in use at multiple purchaser sites. All purchaser sites may not have the same version of the product or the same versions of other third-party products that the product being maintained by the supplier must be integrated with. This information is important if a supplier is going to release a product that must be integrated with different versions of other products at various purchaser sites.

Means to ensure: There should be a database showing what products and version of the product are installed at each purchaser site. Changes must be made against the version of the product in use at the purchaser site for which the release is intended. Before a product is released it must be tested against the versions of the third-party products that exist at the intended purchaser site. Both the supplier and the purchaser must work together to maintain the accuracy of information on this database and it should form the basis of a test plan for each release.

15

Configuration Management

Section 6 of the guideline is entitled: "Quality System—Supporting Activities (Not Phase Dependent)." The previous sections of the guideline have discussed the engineering activities required to develop and test a product. Section 6 discusses the engineering activities that support the development of the product. The following chapters address these activities starting with configuration management.

Configuration management is the process by which a product's baselines (e.g., requirements, source code, test cases, test results, user documentation, etc.) are identified and changes to those baselines are controlled. The guideline identifies the need for an engineering organization to identify, define, and plan for

identification of product baselines,

version control of the product baselines,

roles and responsibilities of the engineering organizations in the change process,

change control procedures, and

status of the change control processes and baseline products.

Configuration management is an extremely important process within software engineering and will be closely audited during the certification process. Chapter 23 takes a more detailed look at configuration management.

6.1   Configuration Management

6.1.1   General

Configuration management provides a mechanism for identifying, controlling and tracking the versions of each software item. In many cases earlier versions still in use must also be maintained and controlled.

Comment: Configuration management is the central management process by which control of the development and maintenance processes is maintained through the control of product and project baselines. Schedules are slipped and budgets are overrun when there is a failure to update schedules and budgets to account for changes in the product or project baselines.

The term "software item" is too limiting concerning what needs to be controlled. Rather the guideline should speak to the control of a project's baselines. A baseline is a product that more than one organization or group will base its work or expectations upon. Generally, any document that has been reviewed and approved for use by other organizations (internal or external) is a baseline. Examples of baselines are contracts, system specifications, software requirements specifications, external interfaces, and user interfaces. When a product or component of the product has been tested and is ready for further testing or for use by the user, then it too is a baseline. Test cases and test results themselves are baselines since they will be used to prove that a product meets requirements and, quite possibly, they will be used as the product goes through maintenance and enhancements.

Changes to these baselines must be approved and coordinated by the various organizations that are impacted by those changes. A configuration control board (CCB) made up of all interested parties (e.g., customer, marketing, test, development, and documentation) is the forum where deliberations concerning changes to baselines take place and where consensus concerning the changes is reached.

The configuration management system should

a) identify uniquely the versions of each software item;

Reason: A software product, and even its components, could have multiple versions based on major and minor releases. Each one of these versions may be maintained as separate products since the purchaser may be using more than one version of the product at different purchaser sites.

Means to ensure: The supplier must have a consistent and documented naming or numbering scheme that is centrally controlled. This scheme must be applied to all items that make up a software product to include software source code modules, documentation, test cases, test results, etc.

b) identify the versions of each software item which together constitute a specific version of a complete product;

Reason: A software product is made up of a number of different documents and software items or modules. Items making up a product release may have different levels of versions due to the number of changes that each individual item has undergone.

Means to ensure: Each software product needs a version description document that identifies the version of the product being released and all the product's components with their individual version numbers.

c) identify the build status of software products in development or delivered and installed;

Reason: Different tools (compilers, linkers) and different environments (operating systems, environment parameters) can be used to build a product at different stages of a product's life cycle. Build records, which document the tools and environment used to build the product as well as the software items that constitute the "as built" product, need to be created, reviewed, controlled, and audited.

Means to ensure: The SPH should state the need for build records to be created and maintained. These records should be identified in the development and maintenance plans as a configuration item.

d) control simultaneous updating of a given software item by more than one person;

Comment: This is very much a management issue that needs to be addressed. The manner in which management wants this issue dealt with needs to be documented in the configuration management plan and the SDP. For instance, project management could dictate that one engineer can have write access to a software item, and that no other engineer could update the item until the first engineer's updates are tested and become part of the product's baseline.

Reason: When several engineers are working on the same module, one engineer's work could overwrite the work of the others, leaving the product in an inconsistent state.

Means to ensure: Source Code Control Systems (SCCSs) can be configured so that a software item can be checked out for updating by only one engineer. SCCSs can also be configured to allow simultaneous updating with the merging of updates performed by the SCCS. During the merging of two versions of a module, human intervention is required when the merge process shows the same line of code changed by two or more engineers.

e) provide coordination for the updating of multiple products in one or more locations as required;

Comment: In some cases, coordination for updating of multiple products may be considered the responsibility of the purchaser, with the supplier providing support. The level of supplier support must be identified in the contract and costed by the supplier.

Reason: Once a product is delivered to a purchaser, it may be installed at multiple sites. As the product matures and further product releases are made less frequently, the purchaser may require that all sites be on the same version. The more sites using the product, the greater the coordination effort and supplier support required.

Means to ensure: The maintenance contract should state that the supplier and the purchaser must work together to maintain a list for each purchaser location that identifies the products, product version, and key contacts. The purchaser and supplier must also work together to identify the schedules and proliferation plans for sites that are to receive product updates.

f) identify and track all actions and changes resulting from a change request, from initiation through release.

Reason: Changes can occur from the moment the first baseline is brought under configuration control (e.g., the contract or the System Specification) until the time the product is no longer supported. Making changes to a product baseline is a difficult, time-consuming, and costly process. Changes require coordination of several organizations' efforts, and entail a multistep process. Management must control the change process to ensure that all parties involved are cognizant of the changes taking place, and that they fulfill their responsibility in implementing the changes in an engineering manner.

Means to ensure: The three basic forms used to identify and track actions and changes are Engineering Change Request, Engineering Change Proposal, and Engineering Change Notification.

An Engineering Change Request (ECR), or Problem Report, is a form used by product users, developers, testers, or documenters to report problems or request changes and enhancements. The types of information found on the form would include

originator of report,

problem number,

brief description of problem,

reason for the change,

software element or document affected,

origination date,

priority,

analyst assigned,

date analyst assigned,

date analyst complete, and

Engineering Change Proposal number (optional).

Dates on this form and the ones that follow can use be used to determine how long it takes an organization to respond to engineering change requests and where the bottlenecks are in the process.

An ECR may generate an Engineering Change Proposal (ECP), which describes a change to a baseline product. The analyst assigned to deal with the ECR uses an ECP to identify the proposed change and the cost to implement the change. The types of information found on this form would include analyst,

date submitted,

ECR(s) addressed by ECP,

brief description of proposed change,

modules/documentation/test plans affected,

estimated duration of effort, and

priority.

If, after a review of the ECP, it makes sense to move forward and implement the proposed change, an Engineering Change Notification (ECN) is created. The types of information found this form would include

implementor assigned,

date implementor assigned,

date implementor finished,

ECP addressed by ECN,

brief description of implementation solution,

software affected,

tester assigned,

date tester assigned, and

date tester complete.

6.1.2 Configuration Management Plan

The supplier should develop and implement a configuration management plan which includes the following:

a) organizations involved in configuration management and responsibilities assigned to each of them;

Reason: Configuration management requires the coordination of several organizations (e.g., purchasing, marketing, development, testing, documentation). For these organizations to coordinate their activities, they must understand their role and responsibility and the roles and responsibilities of the other organizations with whom they must interact.

Means to ensure: The SPH defines the roles and responsibilities of the various organizations that must work together to manage changes to a product. In addition, the SPH defines the activities, procedures, and documentation used in controlling the changes to a product. A configuration management plan defines the resources and schedules required to implement the process as defined in the SPH. The plan must be reviewed and approved by the various organizations that must support the activities and products identified in the plan.

b) configuration management activities to be carried out;

Reason: Configuration management is an engineering process whose practices, procedures, and activities need to be identified and planned to allow the various organizations that have a responsibility for implementing the plan to cost and schedule the effort in order to meet their responsibilities.

Means to ensure: The requirement for a configuration management process is identified in the Quality Policy. The SPH defines the configuration management practices and procedures as well as the templates for the forms to be used in support of that process. The SDP, or the maintenance plan for products already delivered to the purchaser, identifies a configuration management plan as a subordinate plan. The configuration management plan identifies the product and project baselines as well as the activities, budgets, resources, and schedules that needed to manage those baselines. Senior management reviews the development or maintenance plan to ensure that the configuration management process is in place to support a product's development or maintenance.

c) configuration management tools, techniques and methodologies to be used;

Reason: Implementing configuration management requires forethought concerning tools, techniques, and methodologies. The tools should be purchased, and training in the use of the tools, techniques, and methodologies must take place before the configuration management activities begin.

Means to ensure: The configuration management plan should identify, cost, purchase, and prototype the use of the tools, techniques, and methodologies that are to be used to support the configuration management process.

d) the stage at which items should be brought under configuration control.

Reason: This is an extremely important decision. When, in the overall project schedule, an item gets baselined has an effect on various organization's budgets and schedules. The costs of making changes to controlled (baselined) items is much greater than the cost of making changes to non-baselined items. Bringing components under control too soon means that changes to the components will be costly to other organizations that have based some or all of their work on the component. Bringing a component under control too late impacts the other organizations' schedules and the quality of their work, since those organizations' schedules may become squeezed while they wait for a product they need to be baselined.

For example, the testing organization cannot start testing an item until it is baselined nor can technical publications complete the user manuals until the user interface has been baselined. If either or both organizations begin creating test cases or documentation on a non-controlled or non-baselined user interface, they run the risk of having to rework their documentation or test cases as the user interface undergoes changes during development.

Means to ensure: The SPH should identify which items are to be brought under control when describing the outputs of the various steps that make up the engineering process. The SDP for a specific project identifies the schedule for when these items are to brought under configuration control. Status reports for those items need to state whether these items have been brought under control. Both project and organizational management can use this status as a means to determine if a project is on track.

6.1.3 Configuration Management Activities

6.1.3.1 Configuration Identification and Traceability

The supplier should establish and maintain procedures for identifying software items during all phases, starting from specification through development, replication and delivery. Where required by contract, these procedures may also apply after delivery of the product. Each individual software item should have a unique identification.

Comment: Configuration management is the central control process for the entire product process used to develop or maintain a product. There are many items that need to be separately identified and controlled ranging from high-level specifications to source and compiled software modules as well as test cases and test results. Several organizations may have responsibility for the development, test, or use of these items. For these reasons, a straightforward and consistent naming and numbering convention must be used to support development, test, maintenance, and use of these items.

Procedures should be applied to ensure that the following can be identified for each version of a software item:

a) the functional and technical specifications;

Reason: Engineering efforts are based upon specifications. A software product life cycle generally allows for several versions of the product to be released. As versions of the product are released, new versions of the engineering specifications need to be created that reflect the changes found in the new version of the product.

Means to ensure: The configuration plan should have a name and numbering system for versions of products and the products' baselines.

b) all development tools which affect the functional and technical specifications;

Comment: We feel that the guideline should really be describing all development tools (e.g., linkers, compilers, test tools) on the project that affect the software product itself. But if development tools (e.g., word processors, CASE tools) are used to develop specifications, then they should be identified along with the other development tools.

Reason: During the development and maintenance of a product, the versions of the development tools must be controlled. For instance, compilers, linkers, operating systems, and even the automated configuration management tools themselves need to be controlled. This control is needed to ensure that if a product is reworked or re-created, using a newer version of the development tool (e.g., compiler, linker, automated testing) does not compromise the integrity of that particular version of the product.

Means to ensure: The SPH should state that tools used in the development of a product are to be part of the configuration control process. The SDP should identify development tools by name and version as well as the way in which newer versions of these tools will be managed. The configuration management plan should identify the procedures used to support the use of new versions of the development tools.

c) all interfaces to other software items and to hardware;

Reason: A software product is, in many cases, required to interface with other software products (e.g., operating systems, relational databases, graphical packages, and so on) or to specific hardware platforms. Any change to these interfaces may, and most likely will, cause an impact on the software product as well as on the project's budget and schedule.

Means to ensure: The products that make up the software and hardware platform configuration, and their version identification, must be identified in the contract as well as the baseline product description. The configuration management plan should identify these configurations as part of the product and project baselines. The configuration management plan and contract should state that any changes to these items must be approved by the configuration control board.

d) all documents and computer files related to the software item.

Reason: This is an open-ended statement that needs to be defined by the supplier or by the purchaser in the purchaser/supplier contract. There are a large number of documents and computer files related to the software item but only those items that are directly related to the product baselines (e.g., specification, code modules, test cases, test results, ECRs, ECPs, ECNs, etc.) need be under configuration control.

Means to ensure: The SPH should identify the categories of product and project baselines that are to be under configuration management. The configuration management plan should identify by name the discrete product and project baselines based on the SPH, purchaser requirements specification, purchaser contract, and Statement of Work. As the pieces of composite baselines (e.g., software modules, test cases, change requests) pass verification or validation checks, they are brought under configuration control.

The identification of a software item should be handled in such a way that the relationship between the item and the contract requirements can be demonstrated.

For released products, there should be procedures to facilitate traceability of the software item or product.

Reason: Many times, a product is delivered that has "missed" one or more requirements, or the product may have "undocumented features" that were not required by the purchaser. Missed requirements or undocumented features have a negative impact on the product's quality as well as the project's budget and schedule. In addition, it is a strong indicator of an uncontrolled software process.

Means to ensure: One of the key tools in software engineering is the traceability matrix. A traceability matrix is a multicolumn matrix that traces requirements to design modules, requirements to test cases, and design modules to software modules. This tool, combined with a thorough review process, minimizes the risk of missed requirements or undocumented features.

Requirements Traceability Matrix

Contract Req.	S/W Req.	Design Module	S/W Module
1.1 aaaa	3.1 xxxx	D_Name_1	Module_1
	3.4 xxxx	D_Name_2	Module_2
	7.1 xxxx	D_Name_8	Module_7
1.1.1 aaaa	3.4 xxxx	D_Name_2	Module_3
	6.3 xxxx	D_Name_6	Module_8
9.9.9 aaaa	4.4 xxxx	D_Name_3	Module_10
	5.6 xxxx	D_Name_4	Module_9

Test Traceability Matrix

Contract Req.	S/W Req.	Test Case	S/W Module
1.1 aaaa	3.1 xxxx	T_Name_1	Module_1
	3.4 xxxx	T_Name_1	Module_2
	7.1 xxxx	T_Name_7	Module_7
1.1.1 aaaa	3.4 xxxx	T_Name_1	Module_3
	6.3 xxxx	T_Name_2	Module_8
9.9.9 aaaa	4.4 xxxx	T_Name_2	Module_10
	5.6 xxxx	T_Name_3	Module_9

The purpose of traceability matrices is to ensure completeness in the specification, development, and testing of a product. Each contract requirement must be traced to a software requirement or some other contract deliverable (e.g., documentation, test results, etc.). Each software requirement must be traced to a design module and a test case.

6.1.3.2 Change Control

The supplier should establish and maintain procedures to identify, document, review and authorize any changes to the software items under configuration management. All changes to software items should be carried out in accordance with these procedures.

Comment: This section is a repeat of section 6.1.1.f.

Reason: The software items under configuration management undergo changes as new requirements are discovered or bugs are found. Changes to requirements cause changes to design, software, user documentation, and test cases as well as to the plans and budgets used to support the development and maintenance of the product.

Means to ensure: The Quality Policy should state that any changes to product baselines must be reviewed and approved. The SPH defines the change process in its description of configuration control. The SDP references the configuration management plan for the product being developed and that plan describes the activities for implementing the change process identified in the SPH. There should be a process to audit the configuration control activities.

Before a change is accepted, its validity should be confirmed and the effects on other items should be identified and examined.

Reason: In many cases, changing product baselines is a random and haphazard process that, left uncoordinated, results in an unstable product and missed budgets and schedules. One of the main activities of configuration management is to validate change requests and control the processing of those changes to ensure that a change to one module or product does not have an inadvertent impact on another module or product. This process is supported by the procedures involved in the processing of the ECRs, ECPs, and ECNs discussed in section 6.1.1.f.

Means to ensure: The SPH should identify the change evaluation and validation process when describing the configuration management process. The SDP should reference the configuration management plan. The configuration management plan identifies the budget and personnel resources required to implement configuration management of the baselines identified in the plan.

Methods to notify the changes to those concerned and to show the traceability between changes and modified parts of software items should be provided.

Reason: Changes to software items or product baselines usually affect several engineering groups or organizations. For instance, the software test group must be notified of any changes to the software product so that the change can be validated. Field engineers must know the bug fixes or enhancements that are planned for the next release or are incorporated in the current release.

In addition, a change will in many cases affect more than one component. Again, we must emphasize that changes to a product or product baseline require a thorough engineering approach and not just more management but better management.

Means to ensure: The configuration management plan requires a configuration control board made up of representatives from all organizations responsible for the product to meet in order to authorize and validate any change to the product. The supporting documentation for authorization, communication, and validation are the ECRs, ECPs, and ECNs described in section 6.1.1.

6.1.3.3 Configuration Status Report

The supplier should establish and maintain procedures to record, manage and report on the status of software items, of change requests and of the implementation of approved changes.

Reason: Configuration management should be treated like any other development project effort. Change requests should go through an analysis, design, implementation, test, and release process. Both project and organizational-level management have a responsibility to ensure that the configuration management plan is being executed. From these reports, management can determine whether the engineering process is under control and whether the organization is responding to purchaser requests in a timely and accurate manner.

Means to ensure: The Quality Policy should state that change requests must go through an engineering process similar to the development process. The SPH identifies the practices and procedures used to implement the configuration management process. The SPH requires regular reports on the status of the configuration items as well as the number of changes being made against those items. Examples of such reports are

> number of software modules and test cases verified and under control;

> number of engineering change requests opened;

> number of engineering change proposals opened;

> number of engineering change notification opened;

> average time to close all engineering requests, proposals, and notifications; and

> number of all engineering requests, proposals, and notifications opened for 30, 60, 90, or greater than 90 days.

The configuration management plan explicitly defines the configuration management activities, and their budgets, which are identified in the SPH.

16
Document Control

Engineering is a specification-driven process. There are a number of different engineering documents used in the development and maintenance of a software product. The guideline identifies the need for an engineering organization to identify and control the use of those documents. Control is especially important for the initial approval and dissemination of such documents and the authorization and reissue of updated versions.

6.2 Document Control

6.2.1 General

The supplier should establish and maintain procedures to control all documents that relate to the contents of this part of ISO 9000. This covers . . .

Comment: We define document control as the identification (by name and number) of documents essential for the development of the software product and procedures used to manage the update and use of those documents. Document control, as defined in the guideline, overlaps the configuration management process or is in direct support of that process. Consequently the reader will see a large degree of overlap between this chapter and the previous chapter.

a) the determination of those documents which should be subject to the document control procedures;

Reason: Not every document created by the supplier needs to be under document control. Working copies of product design and test cases need not be under control. Status reports, minutes of meetings, and action item lists should be under project management control, but, depending on the formality of the relationship between the supplier and the purchaser, they may not need be under formal document control. The SPH and any other document that identifies an organization's practices, procedures, methodologies, and guidelines belong under document control.

Means to ensure: The SPH identifies the types of documents that belong under document control. The project's SDP explicitly identifies the documents that belong under document control. The document control plan (DCP) identifies the manner in which the documents identified in the SDP as under document control will be distributed, retrieved, and discarded when they become obsolete.

b) the approval and issuing of procedures;

Reason: To avoid confusion and unnecessary delays in development, the individuals, by job function and name, responsible for the accuracy of the documents (often referred to as the owners) need to be identified. These owners approve the original version of the document and any changes to that document, and should be consulted as to when and to whom the documents should be distributed.

Means to ensure: The SPH should identify the job functions that own documents used in the development of the product. The SDP explicitly specifies the owners of the documents. The DCP specifies the approval process for documentation changes, and the manner in which issuing new versions of a document and retrieval of old versions of a document is controlled.

c) the change procedures including withdrawal and, as appropriate, release.

Reason: Engineering documents will undergo a series of changes during the product life cycle. Having several versions of the same document in use may lead to confusion and delay in developing a product; therefore, a conscious effort has to be made to ensure that older versions of a document have been withdrawn. Also, there is the question of the timing of new releases. Newer versions should be released only when the changes they contain take effect and when there are sufficient changes in the document to warrant a new release.

Means to ensure: The SPH identifies the change and withdrawal procedures at a high level. The document control plan defines the implementation of the general guidelines found in the SPH.

6.2.2 Types of Documents

The document control procedures should be applied to relevant documents including the following:

a) procedural documents describing the quality system to be applied in the software life-cycle;

Reason: The quality system (SPH) document describes the processes that should be followed to ensure that the product is developed according to commonly accepted engineering practices and procedures. Obviously, this document cannot undergo unauthorized changes or be allowed to have out-of-date copies in use.

Means to ensure: In the Quality Policy, identify the individual by name, title, and position who has the sole authority for approving changes to this document. There needs to be a non–project-specific document control plan, at the organizational level, that deals with the organizational-level documents. This plan identifies these documents and the procedures for releasing new versions and withdrawing old versions of this document.

b) planning documents describing the planning and progress of all activities of the supplier and his interactions with the purchaser;

Comment: The phrase "all activities of the supplier" is too general. Interactions with the purchaser (minutes of meetings, contracts, etc.) should be under control depending on the formality of the relationship between the supplier and the purchaser. Planning, status, and progress reports more likely belong under project management control, without the administrative overhead involved with formal document control.

Reason: All interactions with the purchaser should be documented and under document control, since they may be used to settle disagreements with the purchaser.

Means to ensure: The SPH identifies the types of documents that should be under document control. The SDP should identify those documents required by the purchaser that should be under document control as well as the instances of documents identified by the SPH. The DCP describes the plan to control changes to and distribution of these documents. The DCP should be reviewed and authorized by both project and organizational management.

c) product documents describing particular software product, including

— **development phase inputs,**

— **development phase outputs,**

— **verification and validation plans and results,**

— **documentation for purchaser and user,**

— **maintenance documentation.**

Reason: These documents form the basis of the development effort and there must be a process to support their maintenance and distribution. Changes to their contents cannot be unilateral. Changes must be reviewed, authorized, and distributed in a control manner to the organizations affected by the change.

Means to ensure: The SPH should identify these types of documents as controlled documents and describe, in general, the procedures used to control changes to their contents. The SDP explicitly identifies the documents and DCP identifies in detail the resources required to implement the control procedures.

Comment: An organization's Quality Policy, SPH, and procedures should all be under document control.

6.2.3 Document Approval and Issue

All documents should be reviewed and approved by authorized personnel prior to issue. Procedures should exist to ensure that

a) the pertinent issues of appropriate documents are available at appropriate locations where operations essential to the effective functioning of the quality system are performed;

Reason: Documents are often stored in a central location and may not be easily accessible to project members. Engineering documents support the development and test efforts. These documents must be available for use by those engaged in developing and testing of the product. This is a key part of the ISO guideline and will be closely audited.

Means to ensure: The Quality Process should state that documents related to process quality or describe the process must be available to the staff. The SPH identifies the types of documents that should be available to engineers. The DCP should identify where these documents are stored and how they can be obtained or how they are to be distributed. The procedure for obtaining the documents should facilitate their retrieval and use. Management, via process quality audits, should conduct periodic audits to ensure that the project has the latest versions of any needed engineering document and knows how to access the versions of documents needed to perform its tasks.

b) obsolete documents are promptly removed from appropriate points of issue or use.

Reason: Obsolete documents, such as out-of-date design documents, test cases, and development plans, can cause confusion and create problems if they continue to be used.

Means to ensure: The SPH should state that obsolete documents are to be withdrawn from use. The document control plan should identify procedures for withdrawing any outdated documents from each department. Management should ensure that everyone affected is aware of these procedures, so that when a new copy of any document arrives, the old copy is discarded or withdrawn immediately according to preestablished rules. Prior versions of documents should be kept under document control to serve as project "history," but prior versions should not be allowed to exist in the general work areas. Management should conduct reviews regarding the handling procedures for obsolete documents and periodically perform a self-audit to ensure that these procedures are followed.

Where use is made of computer files, special attentions should be paid to appropriate approval, access, distribution and archiving procedures.

Reason: Many organizations implement a paperless documentation system and the control of these on-line documents require different procedures than hard copies of documents. When files are stored on-line, appropriate measures should be taken, so that only one individual has update capability for these documents while allowing many to have access to the document. Any updates to the document should be reviewed and authorized by the document owner and possibly management. In addition, there should be safeguards to ensure that the documents are not lost due to system failure.

Means to ensure: The DCP should identify the approval, access, distribution, and archiving procedures used to manage the documents that are on-line. Management should review the plan, and audits of the documentation control procedures should be performed.

6.2.4   Document Changes

Changes to documents shall be reviewed and approved by the same functions/organizations that performed the original review and approval unless specifically designated otherwise. The designated organizations shall have access to pertinent background information upon which to base their review and approval.

Reason: Software development is actually an engineering research and development effort. The documents that support this effort undergo changes as the development effort uncovers new information. Before changes are made, the authors/owners of the document should review the change to ensure that the proposed change is necessary as well as complete and accurate.

Means to ensure: In the SPH, specify that original authors must review any proposed changes unless the original authors are specifically relieved of this responsibility. In the SDP, identify by name, position, function, and organization the authors of the specific documents. When the original authors are no longer responsible for the document, then the SDP should identify the new individual responsible for the document. The DCP should identify the procedures to be used to route the changes to the authors and people who were involved in the original approval and review of the documents. The author/owner review and approval/disapproval of the changes should be documented.

Where practicable, the nature of the change shall be identified in the document or the appropriate attachments.

Comment: The key word here is "practicable." The guideline suggests that a change history be kept with the document. An organization should use its own judgment in this case.

Reason: Users of a document may obtain a better understanding of the document if they can follow the evolution of the changes made to the document. Also, a history of the changes allows for an audit to be performed to ensure that the changes were accurate and authorized.

Means to ensure: The SPH should require that a history of document changes be either kept in the document, attached to the document, or referenced by the document as being in another document or computer file. The DCP should describe the specific mechanisms used to maintain a history of the changes in a project's documents.

A master list or equivalent document control procedure shall be established

to identify the current version of documents in order to preclude the use of non-applicable documents.

Reason: A master list identifies the documents that are applicable for a specific project. This list must also identify the current version for each document. This list allows for a single, coherent, identification and version description for all the documentation used to support the development and maintenance of a software product.

Means to ensure: The SPH should state that a master list of documents is required for each project. The DCP identifies the documents that belong on the list and the owner of the list. For each item on the list the following information should be maintained:

> name of the document,
>
> version number of the document,
>
> date of release,
>
> location,
>
> author,
>
> owner (or author's manager),
>
> reviewers, and
>
> approval authority.

Documents shall be reissued after a practical number of changes have been made.

Reason: It's not feasible to reissue documents after each and every change. Therefore, when a significant number of changes have been made, incorporate these changes into the document and reissue the document.

Means to ensure: The SPH should state that documents shall be reissued based on the judgment of the document's owner and on review by the owner's manager. The document control plan should restate the policy found in the SPH.

17

Quality Records

Engineering organizations should maintain records that document the quality of their processes and products. Records of changes to baselines, reviews, audits, and test results should be maintained. The guideline suggests that procedures and processes should be identified and implemented to control the accumulation, storage, and retrieval of such documents.

6.3 Quality Records

The supplier shall establish and maintain procedures for identification, collection, indexing, filing, storage, maintenance and disposition of quality records.

Quality records shall be maintained to demonstrate achievement of the required quality and the effective operation of the quality system. Pertinent subcontractor quality records shall be an element of these data.

Comment: The guideline is speaking of two types of quality here: process quality and product quality. Process quality is determined through audits (verification) of the engineering process. Product quality is determined through testing (validation) the product.

Reason: Putting an engineering process in place to develop software does not guarantee that the process will be followed or is effective. Checks (e.g., audits, reviews, and tests) must be performed to ensure that the process is being applied and that the process is achieving the product's quality goals. Quality records are the result of these checks. These records need to be kept for process and product improvement.

Means to ensure: The SPH identifies the checks that verify the implementation of the organization's engineering processes and validate the products generated by that process. The SPH should also identify the procedures and forms used to support these checks and the type of information produced by these checks that need to be retained. The SDP and subordinate plans identify the budget and schedule for these checks. The SDP and DCP identify the procedures used to store and maintain the output of these checks.

All quality records shall be legible and identifiable to the product involved.

Reason: Quality records are engineering documents. For these documents to be useful in supporting product and process improvements, they must be legible and traceable to the product and the step used to create the product that the review or audit process was verifying.

Means to ensure: The SPH should define templates for review, audit, walk-through, and test reports. These templates can be tailored for individual projects, but they should include fields that identify the product being reviewed, audited, or tested.

Quality records shall be stored and maintained in such a way that they are readily retrievable in facilities that provide a suitable environment to minimize deterioration or damage and prevent loss.

Reason: These records will be used to verify that an engineering process is followed and that the product meets the purchaser's requirements. They will also serve as a basis for product and process improvement. In the case of test results, they can be used to prove that tests were run and the component/product was found fit for use. These records will be used for some period of time beyond the product or project life span; therefore, a conscious effort must be made to maintain these records.

Means to ensure: The entire purpose of the guideline is to ensure that an organization is following an engineering process in the development of products. The SPH should state that records proving the use of this process shall be kept. In addition, the SPH should identify the format for the records. The document control plan or configuration management plan should identify the manner in which these records are to be gathered, stored, and retrieved for use.

Retention times of quality records shall be established and recorded.

Reason: Like many organizations, everyone wants to collect data but no one thinks about getting rid of it. A determination should be made concerning how long the data need to be kept. The time frame could extend well beyond the end of the product lifetime in the cases of test cases and test results.

Means to ensure: The SPH should give some broad general guidelines concerning retention time for quality records. The project's DCP should explicitly identify the retention time for each type of documentation and the procedures for purging the documents.

When agreed contractually, quality records shall be made available for evaluation by the purchaser or his representative for an agreed period.

Reason: Where the price of product failure is high, the purchaser would be wise to require the right to audit the supplier's process verification records and the product validation records to ensure that sound software engineering practices and procedures are being used in the development of the product.

Means to ensure: Identify in the contract the categories of records that must be supplied for purchaser audits. The SDP should identify these records by name and the document control plan should identify procedures used to control these named documents.

18

Measurement, Rules, and Tools

Engineering management should be a closed-loop process where measurements are taken to determine the quality of the products and processes used to create or manage those products. The guideline states that product measurement is based upon purchaser/customer feedback and a need to capture and use those measurements for product improvement. The guideline suggests that process measurement is used to determine whether schedule milestones are being met and whether the by-products of the process are meeting their quality goals. The guideline points out that for measurements to be useful, an organization needs to identify the current level of performance, improvement goals, measurement data to be collected, and actions to be taken based on measuring data against goals.

This chapter also addresses sections 6.5, Rules, Practices and Conventions, and 6.6, Tools and Techniques. The guideline is very brief in its discussion of these topics, no doubt due to their obvious nature.

6.4 Measurement

6.4.1 Product Measurement

Metrics should be reported and used to manage the development and delivery process and should be relevant to the particular software product.

There are currently no universally accepted measures of software quality. However, at a minimum, some metrics should be used which represent reported field failures and/or defects from the customer's viewpoint. Selected metrics should be described such that results are comparable.

Comment: To improve the software development process, you must have quantifiable numbers or metrics to determine where improvement can be made in the process. Even though there are no universally accepted measurements of software quality, there are popular measurements used in the software industry. The following are examples of the type of measurements that ought to be considered.

Number of defects: The following is a list of the most common measurements for defects:

total number of defects found,

severity of defect,

time taken to fix the defect,

number of open problems at product turnover time, and

total time taken for test.

Test coverage: Percentage of code covered by system-level tests.

Bad fixes: Number of times the same problem had to be retested.

Number of requirement changes: This is a count of number of additions, changes, and deletions to the requirements after the requirements are approved. The measure reflects the quality of requirements gathering and specification and can be used to determine the system stability. The items that are frequently measured in this category are the type of change (e.g., functionality, technical constraints, environment) and how long after baselining the first version of the purchaser's requirement document was the change introduced.

Work effort: This can be measured in terms of cost, schedule, and performance. Work effort reflects the hours spent on development of a new application or application enhancement, or support and maintenance of an existing application. It is collected during the system development life cycle to provide historical data and improve estimating for future projects. Work effort is used to determine the effectiveness of the planning and managing when actual hours spent is compared to planned hours.

Costs are used to determine the effectiveness of project planning. The data are derived from work effort and includes expenses, for example, hardware, software, travel, supplies, photocopies, etc. The data for schedule are derived from planned start, actual start, planned completion, and actual completion. Schedule data are measured to determine the effectiveness of project planning and managing.

The size measure is important as the cost and amount of effort required to develop a product directly relates to the size of a product. In this category, lines of code and function points are typically used for collecting data. There are no standards for lines of source code in the industry.

Function points are a method for sizing a project based on a user view of external inputs, outputs, inquiries, interface files, and internal logical files. The number of function points that a system has is determined by using the International Function Point User's Group (IFPUG) Counting Practices. The function points are counted based on the following:

Logical internal files: data stored and maintained by system;

External interface files: data passed or shared with other systems;

External inputs: transactions, additions, changes;

External outputs: reports; and

External inquiries: no updates.

Documentation errors: Documentation errors are very common in the software industry. Unfortunately, too little attention is given to errors pertaining to incorrect or missing descriptions of functionality, unclear explanations, spelling, and basic user-friendly issues.

User satisfaction: Software organizations should measure user satisfaction. The data can be collected by written surveys, phone surveys, one-on-one feedback meetings, user group meetings, and site surveys.

The supplier of software products should collect and act on quantitative measures of the quality of these software products. These measures should be used for the following purposes:

a) to collect data and report metric value on a regular basis;

Reason: Software development management needs to be a closed-loop process. Without quantifiable measurements, management can only guess at the need for or the effectiveness of changes made to the engineering process.

Means to ensure: The Quality Policy should dictate the need for a metrics program. The SPH should define what that program is and the procedures to implement the program. A separate metrics plan for each project should identify the resources and activities needed to implement the program. A measurement program should address

what metric is being measured and the reason;

how the data will be collected, used, and reported;

how the corrective action will be selected and implemented;

what procedures will be followed to determine if the corrective action has addressed the problem.

b) to identify the current level of performance on each metric;

Reason: The current level is the starting point (i.e., baseline) for determining the need for improvements and measuring the impact of the improvements that are applied.

Means to ensure: Perform the measurement and document the result for each activity and product being measured according to the practices and procedures defined in the metrics plan.

c) to take remedial action if metric levels grow worse or exceed established target levels;

Reason: There needs to be more to a metrics program than just gathering metrics. Metrics programs must be coupled with management action based on the information provided by such a program. There must be a "trigger" that causes management to react when a measurement fails to meet or exceeds established target levels.

Means to ensure: The Quality Policy should state the need for management review and action based on the information provided by the metrics program.

d) to establish specific improvement goals in terms of the metrics.

Reason: Metrics are used to support management decisions. Many times a metrics program is put in place without forethought as to what the end result of the metrics gathering is to be.

Means to ensure: A metrics plan should determine what is the goal and what is to be measured, identify the data to be gathered, define the data unambiguously, gather data, use realistic measurement criteria, and take corrective actions for improvement.

6.4.2 Process Measurement

The supplier should have quantitative measures of the quality of the development and delivery process. These metrics should reflect

a) how well the development process is being carried out in terms of milestones and in-process quality objectives being met on schedule;

Reason: Even if an organization has a defined engineering process there must be project reviews to ensure the engineering process is being followed, the project is on schedule, and that the products of that process are meeting their quality goals.

Means to ensure: The Quality Policy should state that all projects must use the practices and procedures found in the SPH. The SPH identifies the engineering practices, procedures, reviews, and tests to be performed. The SDP identifies the products, the budgets, and the schedules for in-process reviews, audits, and tests used to determine to what degree budget, schedule, and product quality goals are being met. Data from these reviews should be summarized and presented in order to determine to what degree the engineering process is affecting the development efforts and the quality of the product.

b) how effective the development process is at reducing the probability that faults are introduced or that any faults introduced go undetected.

Comment: This section is a summary of the entire metrics program.

Here, as for product metrics, the important thing is that levels are known and used for process control and improvement and not what specific metrics are used. The choice of metrics should fit the process being used and, if possible, have a direct impact on the quality of the delivered software. Different metrics may be appropriate for different software products produced by the same supplier.

Reason: The guideline points out that the engineering process should be measured to determine its effectiveness in reducing faults in the product with the purpose of developing more reliable, meaning quality, products. An engineering organization should perform frequent testing, reviews, and audits to detect errors and nonconformance throughout the development or maintenance cycle, thus minimizing or eliminating the impact of errors on the process and the project itself. An organization needs to check to ensure that what is being measured is what needs to be measured in order to determine what process improvements have a positive effect on the quality of the product.

Means to ensure: The selection of appropriate metrics is an important step. The answer to the question, "Why are you measuring this and what are you going to do with the measurement?" is the key to selecting a measure.

6.5   Rules, Practices and Conventions

The supplier should provide rules, practices and conventions in order to make the quality system specified in this part of ISO 9000 effective. The supplier should review these rules, practices and conventions and revise them as required.

Comment: This blanket statement can be read to mean that supplier management has ensured that methodologies, practices, and procedures are in place so that the engineering process identified in the SPH can be implemented. Therefore, an engineering organization will need to define the manner in which it performs analysis, design, testing, configuration management, maintenance, reviews, inspections, costing, and scheduling. These are all lower-level documents than the SPH. The SPH says what has to be done; these rules, practices, and conventions say how. Defining how is beyond the scope of the guideline.

6.6   Tools and Techniques

The supplier should use tools, facilities and techniques in order to make the quality system guidelines in this part of ISO 9000 effective. These tools, facilities and techniques can be effective for management purposes as well as for product development. The supplier should improve these tools and techniques as required.

Comment: This is another blanket statement pointing out the obvious. The guideline has described generic engineering management and development processes and is now recommending that tools, facilities, and techniques be identified to implement those processes.

19
Purchasing and Including Third-Party Products

This chapter addresses the issues concerning the purchase and inclusion of third-party products into the supplier's product. In this and the following section the guideline points out that, concerning subcontractors used by the supplier, the supplier should apply many of the same management and engineering techniques as the purchaser uses in relation to the supplier. For example, the supplier should ensure the subcontractor's ability to perform the contracted work and validate the subcontractor's products. Basically, concerning third-party products, the supplier has now become a purchaser in the sense that the supplier must now perform analysis of vendor engineering capabilities, validation of third-party products, and configuration control of included products.

6.7   Purchasing

6.7.1   General

The supplier should ensure that a purchased product or service conforms to specified requirements.

Purchasing documents should contain data clearly describing the product or service ordered. The supplier should review and approve purchasing documents for adequacy of specified requirements prior to release.

Note 7   A purchased product may be a software and/or hardware item intended for inclusion in the required end product or a tool intended to assist in the development of the required product.

Reason: Any purchased item included in the final product or used for development affects overall product quality and behavior. The supplier must ensure that purchased items or services meet the supplier's specifications. The same practices and procedures that the purchaser and supplier use to ensure agreement concerning requirements and acceptance testing should apply to any product developed or service supplied by a subcontractor and used by the supplier in the final product delivered to the purchaser.

Means to ensure: The supplier's SPH should identify the practices, procedures, and activities used to ensure the quality of any purchased product. This effort should mirror the same approach taken by the purchaser and the supplier when they identify purchaser requirements and perform acceptance testing of the product delivered by the supplier, with the difference now being that the supplier is the purchaser and the subcontractor is the supplier.

6.7.2   Assessment of Sub-Contractors

Comment: Again, the guideline is pointing to the need for a supplier to take the same care in selection of subcontractors that the purchaser takes in selecting a supplier.

The supplier shall select sub-contractors on the basis of their ability to meet sub-contract requirements, including quality requirements. The supplier shall establish and maintain records of acceptable sub-contractors.

Reason: The supplier is responsible for the quality of a subcontractor's work. The guideline suggesting the subcontractor's ability to meet requirements and the subcontractor's engineering process should be used to determine whether the supplier engages the subcontractor to deliver a product or service.

Means to ensure: The supplier's SPH should require an analysis to be performed by the supplier of the subcontractor's technical capabilities and engineering process maintenance records for those subcontractors judged capable of meeting the supplier's quality requirements.

The selection of sub-contractors and the type and extent of control exercised by the supplier shall be dependent upon the type of product and, where appropriate, on records of sub-contractor's previously demonstrated capability and performance.

Reason: The supplier should base its selection of subcontractors and the level of control over the subcontractor that is needed to ensure the quality of the subcontractor's product upon the type of product and the subcontractor's demonstrated capability. The product could be a commercially available off-the-shelf software that is widely used, has a reputation for quality, and is well supported by the developer. Little control is needed in that case. At the other end of the spectrum is a product that is being developed by a subcontractor who has exhibited a lack of engineering ability and lack of quality in the development of previous products. In cases like these, the supplier should take proper contractual precautions and exercise a greater level of control over the subcontractor.

Means to ensure: The supplier's SPH should identify a process by which a subcontractor's products, engineering process, and support capability are analyzed to determine the level of control required to ensure the delivery of quality product from the subcontractor. We suggest that the guideline be used as a baseline for discussions and contract between the supplier and subcontractor.

The supplier shall ensure that quality system controls are effective. (ISO 9001:1987, 4.6.2)

Reason: The supplier is responsible for any product or service included in the product or service that the supplier deliveries to the purchaser. The fact that a supplier has subcontracted work to a third party does not relieve the supplier of any contractual obligations between the supplier and the purchaser that concern the quality of any component of the final, integrated product.

Means to ensure: The supplier should state in the contract with the subcontractor that there are to be reviews and audits of the subcontractor's products and processes as well as acceptance testing by the supplier of products delivered by the subcontractor. The supplier's SPH should state that this is part of the engineering process, and the supplier's SDP should identify the plans to carry out these activities.

6.7.3 Validation of Purchased Product

The supplier is responsible for the validation of sub-contracted work. This may require the supplier to conduct design and other reviews in line with the supplier's own quality system and, if so, such requirements should be included in the sub-contract. Any requirements for acceptance testing of the sub-contracted work by the supplier should be similarly included.

Reason: If the quality of one of the components that is subcontracted is poor, the whole product is affected. The supplier should ensure that the subcontractor performs quality control– and quality assurance–related activities and if necessary require joint reviews during development of subcontracted products. Once again, the degree of control that the supplier should have over the subcontractor will vary from one subcontractor to another based upon a combination of the criticality of the product or service and the subcontractor's reputation.

The supplier's acceptance criteria for the subcontracted work should be communicated to the subcontractor for review and agreement. This helps minimize misunderstandings between the supplier and subcontractor if and when a subcontractor's product fails an acceptance test.

Means to ensure: The supplier's requirements, along with the acceptance criteria, should be clearly stated to the subcontractor in the contract negotiations. Any specific quality-related efforts the supplier requires from the subcontractor (e.g., reviews and audits) should be specified in the contract.

Where specified in the contract, the purchaser or his representative should be afforded the right to determine at source, or upon receipt, that purchased product conforms to specified requirements. Validation by the purchaser may not absolve the supplier of the responsibility to provide acceptable product nor may it preclude subsequent rejection.

Reason: The purchaser may determine that a test of a subcontractor's product by the purchaser is warranted. This desire on the part of the purchaser can be based on the criticality of the subcontractor's product, doubts concerning the subcontractor's engineering capabilities, and doubts concerning the supplier's ability to test the product.

Means to ensure: The contract between the purchaser and supplier should state that the purchaser has the right to test a subcontractor's product at the subcontractor's facility or upon receipt either by the supplier or the purchaser. The contract should also state that the purchaser's testing or acceptance of a subcontractor's product does not relieve the supplier from responsibility concerning the quality of the product or the cost of any further work needed to ensure that the product meets its requirements.

When the purchaser or his representative elects to carry out validation at the sub-contractor's premises, such validation should not be used by the supplier as evidence of effective control of quality by the sub-contractor.

Reason: A subcontractor's product that passes a purchaser's test is not proof by itself that the subcontractor followed an engineering process in the development of the product or that the product has met requirements. This statement does not relieve the supplier from the responsibility of ensuring that the subcontractor has created a product that meets requirements through the use of an engineering process. If the subcontractor's work is deficient, the supplier is still responsible regardless of whether the purchaser's tests of that product were successful.

Means to ensure: The purchaser should state in the contract that the supplier is responsible for ensuring that any subcontracted work meets requirements regardless of any test, review, or audit performed by the purchaser.

6.8   Included Software Product

A supplier may have third-party products that need to be integrated with its own products. Some of these products may be supplied by the purchaser. The supplier should identify procedures to ensure that these products meet stated quality goals and that the procedures and plans are in place for the storage, protection, and maintenance of the these third-party products.

The supplier may be required to include or use software product supplied by the purchaser or by a third party. The supplier should establish and maintain procedures for validation, storage, protection and maintenance of such product. Consideration should be given to the support of such software product in any maintenance agreement related to the product be delivered.

Purchaser-supplied product that is found to be unsuitable for use should be recorded and reported to the purchaser. Validation by the supplier does not absolve the purchaser of the responsibility to provide acceptable product.

Reason: The supplier may be directed by the purchaser to accept and integrate a third-party product, or one developed by the purchaser, into the product being developed by the supplier. The supplier should validate the third-party product to ensure that the product is reliable and meets its requirements. This validation effort should be agreed to by the purchaser, and the purchaser should bear the costs of the validation effort if the product is being delivered by the purchaser to the supplier.

The supplier is responsible for the storage and the protection of the product. Both the supplier and the purchaser must agree upon a maintenance plan for the third-party product to include bug fixes and enhancements. The original developer is the most likely candidate to maintain the third-party product, but if the purchaser wants the supplier to perform these duties, then the supplier should create a plan that identifies the facilities, resources, hardware, and software required to perform those maintenance efforts.

Means to ensure: The contract should clearly state the purchaser and supplier responsibility concerning the validation, storage, protection, and maintenance of any product that the purchaser requires the supplier to integrate into the product being developed by the supplier. The supplier should develop plans and identify the costs to the purchaser for the validation, integration, and maintenance of third-party products.

20
Training

Engineers need to be trained in order to meet their responsibilities. An engineering organization must identify the techniques, tools, procedures, and methodologies that are used in the development and maintenance of a product. Once these have been identified, then a program can be instituted to ensure that engineers are proficient in their use.

The guideline is a little too narrow in its discussion of training. Earlier, during the discussion of planning or acceptance, there should have been a discussion of the topic of user training, since both the purchaser and supplier will most likely have a shared responsibility for that task.

6.9 Training

The supplier should establish and maintain procedures for identifying the training needs and provide for the training of all personnel performing activities affecting quality. Personnel performing specific assigned tasks should be qualified on the basis of appropriate education, training and/or experience, as required.

The subjects to be addressed should be determined considering the specific tools, techniques, methodologies and computer resources to be used in the development and management of the software product. It might also be required to include the training of skills and knowledge of the specific field with which the software is to deal.

Appropriate records of training/experience should be maintained.

Reason: An engineering organization should identify the techniques, tools, procedures, and methodologies that are used in the development and maintenance of a product. Engineers who lack "hands on" experience with the tools and technologies need to be trained in order to meet their responsibilities. Once these engineers are identified, then a training program can be instituted to ensure that engineers are proficient in their use.

Means to ensure: There are basic engineering skills required of all engineers in addition to project-specific skills. Examples of engineering skills required by all engineers are analysis, design, and test case development. Specific project skills are the programming languages, operating system calls, design methodologies, test tools, and configuration management tools.

We recommend the use of a skills matrix to identify gaps in the engineer's backgrounds that can be filled through a training program. Along the left border of the matrix would be the names of the engineers in the organization or project. Across the top of the matrix would be the skills required. The matrix could be filled in with a "1" if an engineer has actually used the skill, a "2" if the engineer has taken a course in the skill, and a "3" if the engineer has used the skill, or has taken a course in the skill but hasn't used the skill in over 3 years. When complete, the matrix indicates which engineer needs more training as well as serves as a documented baseline for developing a training plan. Records of all training should be kept, reviewed annually (at least), and updated to ensure that an organization's engineers stay current with the technology.

21

The Audit Process

When a company makes the decision to apply for an ISO 9000 registration, it selects a certification body. The selection decision is based on the availability of the auditors, the location of the auditor company, the reputation of the auditors, and the total cost involved in an audit. The amount of time required for an audit will vary depending on the size of the company and the scope of the audit.

Once the certification body is selected, the certification body appoints a lead auditor to go to the company. This lead auditor may also be the team leader. The certification body also assigns other qualified audit team members.

The lead auditor, along with the team members, develops an audit plan that addresses the following:

— the areas of the company that will be audited and the names of the auditors that will be assigned to the respective areas,

— details of the number of days it will take to perform the audit,

— details of individual activities to be performed during the audit, and

— exact agenda that will be followed.

Once the audit is scheduled the company being audited needs to prepare for the audit day. Selected personnel should be available for the auditors to answer any product- or process-related questions or to direct the auditors to the appropriate file or documentation. Specifically, the individual responsible for ensuring the implementation of the Quality Policy, and the project managers, configuration managers, test managers, and software quality assurance engineers should be prepared to be interviewed by the auditors.

The auditors will look for the presence of a layered, documented, engineering process and evidence of its use. The whereabouts of the company's Quality Policy and its basic tenets should be known by every employee. Within the software engineering department all engineers should know the whereabouts and basic tenets of the software process handbook. Project managers should be able to produce requirement documents, implementation plans, test plans, test cases, test results, review reports, contract review minutes, change control documentation, and process verification reports. Configuration managers and documentation managers should be ready to show the "paper trail" that documents the change process and gives evidence of that process being used. Training records should be up to date and tied into the work being required of the engineers. In addition, a quality assurance plan (audits, metrics, etc.) for each project should exist, and evidence that the plan was implemented be ready for the auditors' review.

On the day of the audit, the lead auditor schedules an opening meeting at which he or she introduces the audit team members to the company management and discusses the process of the audit, the specific details on how the audit will be conducted, who will be assigned to various areas, and what type of support will be required from the audited company. The company assigns a guide to the audit team. The individual selected as the guide would have the required knowledge of all the processes and procedures of the company. He or she will assist the auditors to obtain any information required for the audit. The audit team conducts the tour of the site to become familiar with the facilities, departments, and staff members.

During the audit the auditors ensure that the department being audited has all the processes and work instructions documented. In addition, the auditors ensure that these processes and work instructions are being followed on a continuous basis. The auditors also ensure that practices are in compliance with the ISO standard.

Any observations made by the auditors on noncompliance are noted, and written reports are prepared on a daily basis. On a daily basis the audit team holds a meeting during which all the findings are discussed. Any noncompliance findings are discussed with the company guides. If no resolution is found for the noncompliance, agreement regarding the noncompliance is obtained from the guide.

At the end of the audit, a formal closing meeting is conducted with the company management. All the noncompliance events are discussed in detail with the company officials. A final report of the audit findings is prepared and either given at the time of the closing or mailed at a later date. A surveillance audit is scheduled for a later date to ensure that the company has addressed all the noncompliance and has put a process in place to ensure that no additional noncompliance would take place in the future.

22
Specifying the Purchaser Requirements

There is a general recognition that regardless of the development model used, the software life cycle consists of specification, requirements definition, implementation, testing, and maintenance. Each of these phases is meant to address certain questions whose answers will provide the information needed for the next phase to begin. These questions are fairly simple to answer. The key is to make sure that the right questions are asked, of the right people, at the right time, and that the answers are reviewed by the right people.

This chapter takes a detailed look the first two phases of the software life cycle. The reasons for this narrowing of focus is twofold. First, it has been shown time and again that the better we specify the product and define the requirements needed to implement the product, the less time and effort it will take to complete the following phases. Second, it is during these two phases that the purchaser and supplier must come to a common understanding of the product and the costs and risks involved in creating or enhancing a product. Without a common understanding these three organizations are likely to work at cross-purposes, the result being a negative impact on the product's final quality, costs, schedule, as well as the morale within the organization.

For the purpose of this discussion we consider marketing as the "purchaser" and engineering as the "supplier."

The purpose of the Marketing Requirements Document (MRD) or System Specification (SS) is to identify the needs of the customer and the product features to meet those needs, and to arrive at a preliminary estimate of the resources required to create the product. Marketing takes the lead in this effort and is responsible for creating the MRD or SS.

The problems at this stage stem from the fact that in many cases marketing does not always know what it needs to tell engineering that will allow engineering to form a reasonably accurate estimate of what needs to be built. What generally happens is that even if an MRD is written, it's not detailed enough, or if it has enough detail, it has been written in the manner of a Victorian novel, which makes it hard to read and understand.

The MRD or SS can be a fairly simple and straightforward document to create and review. All that needs to be done is to ask the right questions and state the answers in a manner that makes them easy to read, understand, and discuss. The questions that need asking and why they should be asked at this phase are as follows.

The first question to ask is, What is the product and what is its purpose? Marketing needs to briefly state what the product is and its purpose. This description will allow the customer, marketing, engineering, and management to have a common understanding of what is going to be built and why.

What assumptions are there concerning this product? There must be some reasons why marketing thinks people need this product or why the organization would benefit from producing this product. These assumptions need to be validated by management and engineering; otherwise, the product will be based on false premises and most likely fail to be created or fail once it reaches the user.

In what context does this product exist? How does it fit in to the "system"? Marketing, supported by engineering, needs to identify at a high level the source and destination of the product's inputs and outputs so that agreement can be reached between marketing and engineering as to what these interfaces are going to be. Interfaces are probably the most important type of requirement and the ones most costly to add or delete.

What are the functional capabilities of this product? What is it we want it to do? Marketing must provide a brief description of the functional capabilities and the inputs and outputs required by those capabilities. If this type of high-level statement cannot be made in a clear and concise manner, then we run the risk that engineering will misinterpret these capabilities, incorrectly define the requirements needed to implement them, and misjudge the cost in dollars and hours to implement them.

What are the product's technical constraints? Marketing, supported by engineering, must identify the timing, sizing, throughput, and data retention constraints as well as any industry standards that apply to this product. If the constraints are not identified during this phase, then engineering will most likely create a product that is too big, is too slow, or fails to meet whatever standards apply.

What is the configuration that this product must operate within? Marketing must identify the hardware and operating system, third-party software (and version), and the prior releases of the product with which the new product must be compatible.

Who is the user of the product? Marketing is closest to the user, so it must identify the user's level of education, technical background, familiarity with computers, and working environment. This information will have an impact on the sophistication and usability of the product's interface.

How is the user going to use this product? Marketing, supported by engineering, must identify the various tasks for which the user will use the product, how often each task is performed, and the order of importance of the various tasks. This information will impact the product's user interface and reliability as well as help focus the development and testing strategies.

What product documentation is to be supplied? Marketing must identify the customer-related documentation required for this product. This allows technical publications to give a preliminary cost for these documents.

What are the technical risks associated with this product? Marketing and engineering must identify the technical difficulty in developing and marketing the product. Such things as external dependencies and the level of certitude concerning the requirements must be identified, evaluated, and understood so that marketing, engineering, and management can work together to minimize the risk.

There are a number of benefits to be had by answering these questions during this phase. For engineering, the information gained from the answers lays a strong foundation for the requirements definition phase and expedites the effort required for that phase. For management, the information provides the data needed to make a "go/no-go" decision concerning the viability of developing the product. But, to repeat a point made earlier, the most important benefit gained from answering these questions is that purchaser and supplier will now have a common understanding of the product, the customer, the costs, and the risks involved in creating the product.

The second phase is the software requirements definition phase. In this phase engineering refines the capabilities and constraints identified in the MRD or SS and decomposes them into implementation requirements described in the software requirement specification (SRS). The goal of this phase is to identify what has to be done in such detail that the solution can be designed and tested. In addition, detailed budget and schedule for each of the following phases can be determined. The questions that need to be asked and answered during this phase are as follows.

What are the engineering assumptions? Engineering must identify the assumptions on which it will be basing its statement of requirements, costs, and schedules. Examples of this can be the level of engineering talent that the project will require or the availability of hardware and software. These assumptions need to be validated by management and engineering; otherwise, the product will be based on false premises and most likely fail to be created or fail once it reaches the user.

What are the implementation requirements? Engineering must refine the product capabilities identified in the MRD into implementation requirements. These implementation requirements must be costed and traced to a functional capability specified in the MRD or SS. Costing the requirements and tracing them back to a functional capability will allow business-like decisions to be made concerning which requirements are implemented and which are postponed or dropped due to cost or schedule constraints.

What are the derived requirements? Engineering must identify derived requirements that cannot be traced directly to a MRD capability. Examples of these might be the need to use a relational database or to develop a software timer to control software interrupts. Some thought has to be given to identifying these type of requirements so that their development or purchase can be costed in terms of budget and schedule and not come as a surprise later in the development stage.

If the system can be in a number of different states, what functionality exists within each state? Certain applications can be in one of several states. Only a subset of functions may be available within any given state. Engineering, supported by marketing, must identify those requirements that exist in only some states so that the design and test cases can reflect this.

How do the technical constraints apply to implementation or derived requirements? Engineering must identify what technical constraints may apply to specific requirements. These constraints will impact the design and implementation of the product and the manner in which it is tested.

What are the user operations? Engineering, supported by marketing, should refine the user tasks identified in the previous phase into detailed user operations and identify the information needed to perform the operations. This information will form the basis of the user interface design as well as test cases.

What are the external interfaces' detailed definitions? Engineering, supported by marketing, must define the external interfaces identified in the previous phase down to their individual components and the range of values for each of the components identified.

What are the key algorithms needed by this product? Do we really want software engineers calculating federal withholding taxes, missile navigation algorithms, or the routing of phone calls across the nation? Engineering, supported by marketing, must identify these types of algorithms.

What are the error handling requirements? Engineering, supported by marketing, must define what can go wrong with the system and what the system should do when it enters an error state. This needs to be stated so that agreement between the customer and engineering can be gained. In addition, engineering needs this for their test plans, and so does documentation.

How will the requirements be tested? Engineering needs to identify how each requirement will be tested or whether it can be tested. If a requirement cannot be tested, then it needs to be restated so that it can be tested or the requirement needs to be deleted since it can never be proved or disproved that it was actually implemented. The manner in which requirements can be tested falls into one of three categories: demonstration, analysis, and inspection.

The SRS is the most important document produced during either of the first two phases. The product's design, test cases, user documentation, and all development costs and schedules will be based on the information found in this document. The SRS serves as a contract between engineering on the one hand and marketing and management on the other. Any change to this document will almost automatically cause a change to schedule and budget. Most changes are related to product capabilities, interfaces, or configurations and most of these changes could and should have been avoided.

Far too often these questions go unanswered or are postponed without sound engineering or business reasons. When this happens a long and tortuous process begins that burns up dollars and hours debating what features should or should not be in the product, handling "new" requirements as they appear during the life cycle, and justifying or ignoring schedule and budget slips. What is worse, and this is really the bottom line, a large portion of our software engineers' creativity and hard work is spent in an ultimately self-defeating attempt to make up for a lack of judgment and clarity shown during the initial phases of the software life cycle.

23
Configuration Management Process

Software development is by its very nature a research and development effort. Consequently the products and by-products of this effort, especially the requirements, are subject to change. In addition software products are made up of a large number of interdependent components. Changes to these products, by-products, and components are, in many cases, made without updates to the project budget and schedule. This failure to update budgets and schedules is the single greatest cause for late, over-budget, unreliable, or incomplete products.

Configuration management is the central control mechanism for controlling the changes to product and project baselines and ensuring that budgets and schedules are updated when changes occur. This chapter is meant as a brief introduction to configuration management as a process and product quality control tool. Basically, configuration control is the identification, evaluation, approval or disapproval, and coordination of product and project baselines, initial product configurations, changes to formally established baselines, and versions of product configurations. In addition, configuration control is involved with the management of the physical components of the software product by physically controlling the items, building the derived items, and building the final product.

In addition to the information concerning the product's configuration, configuration management can be used to maintain or disseminate information concerning the product's development status, as well as information that would be of interest to those who are responsible for the product's liability (see Figure 23.1).

Configuration management must be tailored for the size of the project, and the bureaucratic aspects of the control process must be minimized. Configuration management should be an integral part of the development process and provide a focal point for issue identification and resolution as well as product and project

FIGURE 23.1. Configuration management.

status. This focal point is the configuration control board (CCB), which is an administrative body that approves, monitors, and controls all changes to the system (all software, hardware, and documentation). All changes to the system must be approved by the key members of the CCB who, generally speaking, are the engineering project manager, test and validation manager, marketing, and software configuration manager, and in some cases the purchaser.

The software configuration manager (SCM) is an extremely important position that requires a high level of technical skill. The SCM requires the technical skill to develop the CM plan, create a library structure to support the CM identification scheme, implement access control procedures to baseline items, support the change control process, generate management and status reports, and manage or support the build and release processing. If done properly, the work performed by the SCM provides the engineering basis for all other engineering efforts and allows the other project participants to concentrate on the technical aspects of product development and maintenance rather than the administrative and coordination headaches involved with change control.

As to the change process itself, it is essential that an analysis of that change is performed and, before implementing the change, that a number of factors are taken into consideration. Factors such as functional aspects of the change, phase of the project, possible alternatives, time and cost of the change, interfaces that may be changed, test provisions and data, documentation requirements, integration and acceptance testing, effects on other (related) products, number of customers who will benefit, and the effect of not implementing the change are all serious considerations that must be taken into account before authorizing a change.

Admittedly, there will be times when changes to a product baseline cannot wait for the full CM/CCB approval and implementation process. This generally happens during system-level integration and testing or when a system-disabling bug is reported from the field. When this situation occurs, a "tiger team" will be put together made up of one or more development and test engineers, a technical manager, and a member of the configuration management staff. Under the direct supervision of a technical manager, this tiger team will fix the problem, install the solution, and ship the fix. The configuration manager keeps track of the fix process so that a paper trail of the fixes and any test, reviews, and authorizations skipped can be implemented when time permits.

There is also the physical management aspects of product control. Managing the product baselines is made up of source code control, document control, library management, and status reporting. The project library is the central repository for all baseline specifications and components that can affect the development and maintenance of the product. The two main issues involved with managing this library are security and integrity. Security must control the read/write access to the product baselines in order to protect against

accidental errors—overwrite or deletion of baseline;

invalid updates—changes that have not been authorized, tested, or approved;

subversion—intentional trying to disrupt development or maintenance; and

espionage—accessing confidential material.

The level of security and CM control will vary depending on the size of the project and the confidentiality of the product. Most operating systems and configuration management tools provide the environment to handle security issues.

To avoid any logical or physical catastrophes, components of the library should be backed up on a regular basis. There should be several generations of backups to protect against a corruption of the latest backup. Backups should be planned and run according to plan to minimize their impact upon development and maintenance. A library backup could be full or partial. A partial backup just makes copies of that which has changed since the previous backup. Backups could be run on weekends or early Monday morning. The number of type of backups performed will be based upon the size and importance of the work being done.

Data that have been determined to be of long-term importance to the organization are maintained for longer periods, possibly years, than the backups normally performed. Examples of these might be test cases, test results, and quality audits. Configuration management should have a plan that identifies these data and the manner in which they are archived, stored, and protected from loss or damage.

The configuration management process generates information that can be used to manage the development and maintenance efforts. Status accounting refers to the collection, formatting, and delivery of management information to the project or product managers. Status accounting reports on the status of all baselined items and any requests for changes to those items. In addition, the following information can be made available through the configuration management process and used to manage both the product and the development and maintenance efforts:

status of an item—untested, tested, approved, integrated;

status of change—reviewed, rejected/approved, assignee, tested, implemented;

item definition—versions, changes to the versions;

item problem reports—number, open, closed; and

causes of change requests—fixes, enhancements, adaptations.

Such an important process as configuration management should be regularly audited. These audits are used to determine compliance with configuration management requirements, validate accomplishment of development requirements, validate product testing, and validate production configuration. A project's configuration management process can be audited by internal software quality assurance personnel, prime contractors, or state, federal, or international agencies.

There are several types of audits. A functional configuration audit is the formal examination of functional characteristics of test data for a configuration item prior to acceptance to verify that the item has achieved the performance required. A physical configuration audit is the formal examination of the "as-built" product configuration against its technical documentation in order to establish the product's actual configuration. The formal qualification review is a formal review to ensure that the quality assurance test has been accomplished and to verify that the items as designed and implemented perform as required by the specification performance requirements.

The configuration management plan (CMP) details how the project's technical products will be managed and the manner in which change to these products will be coordinated and approved. The CMP addresses the responsibilities of all organizations and their interface with the configuration management process, as well as how items are identified, controlled, changed, and statused. Regardless of the size of the project there should be a plan in place at the very beginning of the project and much of the administrative and technical details of that plan exercised before items under control of that plan are developed.

The organization should have a tailorable CMP that each project can use as a baseline for its own CMP. The factors affecting tailoring are project size, project life cycle, type of project, distributed or local development, third-party software, number of items to be managed, number of planned variants, and any imposed industry standards. The following is an outline for a CM plan.

I. Introduction

1.1 Project scope

1.2 Purpose

1.3 Resources needed—people, tools, environment

1.4 Acronyms

1.5 Definitions

II. Organizations (roles and responsibilities in regard to CM)

2.1 Test

2.2 S/W development

2.3 Configuration management

2.4 Program management

2.5 Product management

2.6 Engineering management

2.7 Quality assurance

III. Configuration identification

3.1 System specification

3.2 S/W requirements specification

3.3 Design specification

3.4 Test plans

3.5 Test cases

3.6 Test results

3.7 Configuration identification scheme

    Documents
    Software
    Hardware
    Purchase software

3.8 Configuration definition scheme

    Items
    Components
    Product
    Tools

IV. Configuration control

4.1 General statement—purpose

4.2 Change control process

    Parts turnover—when
    Software problem reports
    Deviations and waivers

In summary we must keep in mind that change is the only constant in the software development effort. There must be a way to manage this change in order to maintain accuracy in costs, schedules, requirements, test, design, and documentation. Configuration management is the establishment of project baselines and the evaluation, coordination, and approval of change to those baselines. Configuration management provides integrity of the development and maintenance environment and of the product, and brings a standard approach backed by systematic procedures that support and help expedite the engineering process.

24

The Software Process Handbook as the Quality Manual

This chapter presents a generic software process handbook. We hope that such a document can form the basis for organizations to create their own handbook. We recommend that the handbook be short enough to be read in about an hour. We also recommend that roughly half of the handbook be given over to engineering specification document templates. A handbook that is too long and detailed may go unread, and one lacking templates will be difficult to implement.

Introduction

1.1. Overview

The software process handbook (SPH) defines a phased approach for the development of well-engineered software. The SPH provides guidelines to be followed in each phase as well and templates for product specifications and development plans. These guidelines describe the inputs, outputs, major activities, and organizations responsible for the work performed during each phase. The guidelines are meant to facilitate software development, increase the quality of the organization's products, and minimize the time and effort required to produce products ready for the marketplace. The phases can be customized for a particular software release; however, the guidelines can be modified only upon the mutual consent of the various organizations responsible for the specification, development, testing, and deployment of the product.

The following is a list of the phases for the product development process and the deliverables expected from each phase or the major processes within the phase:

Phase One: Product specification and planning

   a. Marketing requirements document

   b. Preliminary budgets and schedules

   c. Detailed budget and schedule for Phase Two

Phase Two: Engineering specification and planning

   a. Feasibility prototype (optional)

   b. Software requirements specification

   c. Software development plan

Phase Three: Product design

   a. Software design document

   b. System test specification

Phase Four: Implementation

   a. Code and unit tests

   b. Integration tests

   c. System-level test cases developed

Phase Five: System test

   a. Execute system tests

   b. Baseline system test results

   c. Baseline software products

   d. Updated product documentation

Phase Six: Product evaluation

   a. Alpha evaluation

   b. Beta evaluation

Phase Seven: Product release

   a. Release to manufacturing

   b. Release to customer

Phase Eight: Maintenance/enhancement

The software process requires phases to be completed sequentially, although one phase may begin before the previous phase completes, provided that management approves and has been made aware of any known risks involved in overlapping phases. A phase is considered complete when the objectives of the phase have been met, a review of its products has taken place, and the products have been brought under configuration control.

The following sections describe the phases in detail. The following attachments contain outlines for the specifications and plans required during each phase of the development process.

Phase One: Product Specification and Preliminary Planning

Purpose

To identify the customer's needs, product features to meet those needs, and a preliminary estimate of the resources required to create the product features.

Deliverables

The following products are the outputs of this phase:

Marketing Requirements Document

Preliminary budgets and schedules

Detailed budget and schedule for prototyping and creation of the software requirement specification

Exit Criteria

This phase is complete when the following have been reviewed and, where noted have received signature approval:

Marketing Requirements Document—signature V.P. engineering, V.P. marketing, product manager, engineering leads, sales, field application engineer

Preliminary budgets and schedules for the entire project—reviewed by marketing and engineering management

Detailed budget and schedule for Phase Two—reviewed by engineering management

Description

During this phase, marketing creates a Marketing Requirements Document (MRD) that identifies the user, product functionality, and technical constraints of the product to be created. Engineering reviews this document and responds with a preliminary estimate as to the resources and schedule required to create the product. Based on engineering's preliminary estimates, the marketing requirements may expand or contract until marketing and engineering can agree on a match between the marketing requirements and engineering resources. Engineering also supplies a detailed estimate and resources needed for the next phase.

Step 1. Marketing Requirements Analysis

Purpose:	To identify the product's users, functionality, features, and technical constraints
Inputs:	Market analysis, surveys, customer interviews, etc.
Team:	Primary—marketing and purchaser
	Secondary—engineering, sales, field engineers, application engineers
Users:	Engineering, engineering management
Tasks:	1. Interview the purchaser
	2. Create preliminary MRD
	3. Distribute draft MRDs for review
	4. Review MRD with purchaser and engineering, and identify issues
	5. Resolve issues
	6. Update MRD
	7. Repeat steps 4 through 6 if necessary until purchaser and supplier (i.e., marketing and engineering) agree on requirements, deliverables, cost, and schedule
	8. Obtain signature approval
References:	Attachment A—Marketing Requirements Document template
	Attachment B—Marketing and Engineering Interaction during Phase One
Output:	Marketing Requirement Document
Exit criteria:	Review and signoff by purchaser and supplier (e.g., engineering, marketing, sales, and management) of the MRD

Step 2. Preliminary Budget and Schedules

Purpose:	To give an estimate as to the costs and time required to develop and test the product identified in the MRD; this estimate will help narrow the focus of the MRD and allow more timely and accurate detailed estimates to be made in later steps
Inputs:	MRD, development costs, and schedules from similar products
Team:	Engineering, marketing
Users:	Engineering management, marketing management
Tasks:	1. Review the MRD
	2. Estimate in hours the time required to fulfill each marketing requirement and any derived requirements
	3. Review the estimates with engineering management
	4. Identify issues and modify preliminary estimates
	5. Review the estimates with marketing
	6. Identify issues and revise MRD and preliminary estimates, if necessary
	7. Finalize preliminary estimates
References:	Attachment B—Marketing and Engineering Interaction during Phase One
Outputs:	Finalized preliminary estimates
Exit criteria:	Review and approval of preliminary estimates by marketing and engineering management

Step 3. Phase Two Detailed Estimates of
Software Requirements Specification

Purpose:	To give an estimate as to the costs and time required to develop a detailed software requirements phase
Inputs:	MRD, development costs, and schedules from similar products
Team:	Engineering, marketing
Users:	Engineering management, marketing management
Tasks:	1. Review the MRD
	2. Estimate in hours the time required to fulfill each marketing requirement and any derived requirements
	3. Review the estimates with engineering management
	4. Identify issues and modify preliminary estimates
	5. Review the estimates with marketing
	6. Identify issues and revise MRD and preliminary estimates, if necessary
	7. Finalize preliminary estimates
References:	Attachment B—Marketing and Engineering Interaction during Phase One
Outputs:	Finalized detailed estimates for the following phase
Exit criteria:	Review and approval of preliminary estimates by marketing and engineering management

Phase Two: Engineering Specification and Detailed Planning

Purpose

To identify the software and hardware requirements needed to implement the product features specified in the Marketing Requirements Document and to identify and obtain the resources (e.g., engineering hours, hardware, software, and schedule) needed to construct and test the system that implements the requirements.

Deliverables

The following products are the outputs of this phase:

> Feasibility prototype (optional)
>
> Software requirements specification
>
> Software development plan (SDP), which contains or references:
>
>> Development engineering costs and schedules
>>
>> Documentation plan
>>
>> System test plan
>>
>> Alpha evaluation plan
>>
>> Beta plan

Exit Criteria

This phase is complete when the following have been reviewed and where noted have received appropriate signature approval and/or are brought under configuration control:

> Software requirements specification—signature V.P. engineering, V.P. marketing, project manager, engineering leads
>
> Product development plan—signature V.P. engineering, V.P. marketing, V.P. sales, project manager, engineering leads
>
> Feasibility prototype—reviewed by engineering management

Description

Once the MRD has been reviewed and baselined, engineering creates a software requirements specification, which contains the detailed implementation requirements needed to meet the requirements and constraints found in the MRD. See

Attachment C for the Software Requirements Specification Template. Changes to this template must be by mutual consent of marketing and engineering. During this phase engineering may engage in a feasibility prototype effort in order to obtain a better understanding of the technical aspects of the product to be developed.

Toward the end of this phase a software development plan (SDP) will be created. This plan will use prototypes, prior experience, a baselined MRD, and a preliminary software requirements specification to identify the resources, milestones, and deliverables to be used in the creation of the product. In addition, the SDP will reference the plans to test the product, document the product, and evaluate (alpha and beta) the product. The alpha evaluation plan and beta evaluation plan are part of the software development plan and may be generated during later phases.

This phase is completed when the contents of the software requirements specification and the SDP are reviewed and approved by the V.P of engineering, V.P. of marketing, and the project manager.

Step 1. Feasibility Prototyping (Optional)

Purpose:	To determine product feasibility and/or gain familiarity with new interfaces, tools, platforms, algorithms
Inputs:	MRD, software requirements specification (preliminary)
Team:	Primary—engineering
	Secondary—marketing, quality assurance
Tasks:	1. Identify a candidate for prototyping
	2. Create a subset of requirements
	3. Review with marketing and engineering management
	4. Design
	5. Code
	6. Demonstrate prototype
	7. Review results with customer/marketing/management
	8. Repeat steps 1 through 7 if necessary
	9. For future estimating purposes track:
	a. time expended at design and code
	b. lines of code created
Output:	Prototype results, estimated hours spent designing and coding
Exit criteria:	Review by engineering management

Step 2. Software Requirements Specification

Purpose:	Identify in detail the product's inputs, outputs, and the software and hardware implementation requirements needed to create the product functionality and meet the product's technical constraints
Inputs:	Marketing Requirements Document
Team:	Primary—development engineering
	Secondary—marketing, software quality assurance, technical publications
Users:	Marketing, engineering, software quality assurance, technical publications, engineering management
Tasks:	1. Create the software requirements specification
	2. Distribute draft software requirements specification for review
	3. Review and identify issues
	4. Resolve issues
	5. Update software requirements specification
	6. Repeat steps 1 through 5 if necessary
	7. Deliver software requirements specification to configuration management
References:	Attachment C—Software Requirements Specification template
Output:	Software requirements specification
Exit Criteria:	Review and signoff of the software requirements specification by V.P. engineering, V.P. marketing, V.P. sales, project manager, and project technical leads

Step 3. Software Development Plan

Purpose:	To gain agreement among the various organizations as to the resources and schedule required to develop and evaluate the product as well as the responsibilities of those organizations in the management of this effort
Inputs:	MRD, software requirements specification (preliminary and final), data from prototype, prior experience, and roll-ups of the test plan, documentation plan, alpha evaluation plan, and beta evaluation plan
Team:	Primary—engineering management, software quality assurance, technical publications
	Secondary—marketing
User:	Engineering management, marketing management, sales management, and project manager
Tasks:	1. Estimates hours required for different phases
	2. Determine schedules for each phase
	3. Identify external (third party) dependencies and due dates
	4. Identify internal dependencies and due dates
	5. Identify tracking and statusing mechanisms
	6. Create a draft software development plan
	7. Review draft software development plan
	8. Resolve issues
	9. Update plan
	10. Repeat steps 7 through 9 if necessary
References:	Attachment D—Software Development Plan
Output:	Software development plan
Exit criteria:	Review and signoff by V.P. engineering, V.P. marketing, V.P. sales, project manager, project technical leads

Step 4. Documentation Plan

Purpose:	Describe the technical documents required for the developed product. Outline the content and identify the source material for the document. Identify resources required, schedules, and dependencies.
Inputs:	Marketing Requirement Document Software requirements specification External Interface Document
Team:	Primary—technical publications Secondary—development engineering, test engineering, marketing
Tasks:	1. Identify documents to be created or modified 2. For modified documents, identify sections to be modified 3. Identify source of material for new documents or modifications or previous documents 4. Create outline of new and modified documents 5. Identify resources, risks, schedule, and dependencies for creation of documentation 6. Create draft documentation plan 7. Review, identify issues, resolve issues 8. Obtain signature authority for plan 9. Version control the documentation plan
References:	Attachment H—Documentation Plan Template
Output:	Documentation plan
Exit criteria:	Marketing, engineering, and sales management approval of the documentation plan

Step 5. System Test Plan

Purpose:	Identifies and describes the tests required to ensure that the product has met its functional requirements, performs in the manner described in the product documentation, and meets its technical constraints
Inputs:	Software requirements specification, documentation outline
Team:	Primary—software quality assurance
	Secondary—project technical leads, project manager, documentation manager
Tasks:	1. Identify the hardware and software configuration for the test environment
	2. Describe installation of the products to be tested and controlling the test environment
	3. Describe the individual test cases
	4. Estimate schedule and resources required to
	a. create test cases
	b. run test cases
	5. Create draft system test plan
	6. Review draft
	7. Identify issues
	8. Resolve issues
	9. Baseline the system test plan
References:	Attachment G—System Test Specification Template
Output:	System test plan
Exit criteria:	Review and signoff by V.P. engineering

Phase Three: Product Design

Purpose

Define the functional design, interface design, database design, and error handling design. Identify the test cases and create an outline for all product documents.

Deliverables

The following products are the outputs of this phase:

> Software Design Document

> System-level test case definition

Exit Criteria

This phase is complete when the following have been reviewed and received approval or signature signoff:

> Software Design Document—approval of project engineering lead

> System-level test cases—signature V.P. engineering, director of marketing, project manager, engineering leads

Description

During this phase an architectural, detailed design, user interface, database design, and error handling design are created that will describe the software solution for the requirements specified in the software requirements specification. In addition, system-level test cases identified in the previous phase will be defined in detail.

Step 1. Software Design Document

Purpose:	Design the software product architecture, implementation, error handling, user interface, and database design. Once the design has been implemented the design document should be reissued to reflect the "as-built" design.
Inputs:	Software requirements specification, third-party product documentation (especially interface documents)
Team:	Primary—engineering
	Secondary—quality assurance
Tasks:	1. Decompose system into software programs
	2. Describe the program's inputs, outputs, and processing
	3. Decompose program into implementation modules
	4. Design implementation modules
	5. Describe the error handling design
	6. Describe the database design
	7. Determine error handling needed by the module
	8. Decompose user operations into windows or screens
	9. Determine type and placement of graphical objects representing operational information
	10. Prototype windows and/or screens
	11. Demonstrate/review screens and/or screens to engineering management, project manager, quality assurance, and purchaser
	12. Create software design document
	13. Review software design document for completeness
	14. Identify issues and resolve issues
	15. Obtain signature approval
References:	Attachment E—Software Design Document Template
Output:	Software Design Document
Exit criteria:	Review and signoff by engineering management and, for user interface and error handling, review and signoff by marketing and sales management

Step 2. System Test Specification Description

Purpose:	Describes in detail the tests required to ensure that the product has met its functional requirements, performs in the manner described in the product documentation, and meets its technical constraints
Inputs:	System test plan, software requirements specification, documentation outline
Team:	Primary—quality assurance
	Secondary—development engineering, product manager, documentation manager
Tasks:	1. Define in detail for each system test case:

           a. inputs/outputs
           b. test procedures
           c. expected results
           d. assumptions and constraints
           e. location for inputs/outputs
           f. location of test report

      2. Review draft
      3. Identify issues
      4. Resolve issues
      5. Baseline the system test specification

References:	Attachment F—System Test Specification Template
Output:	System test specification
Exit criteria:	Review and signoff by V.P. engineering, project manager, project technical leads

Phase Four: Product Implementation

Purpose

Implement the software, documentation, and system test designs. Additionally, prove that the software developed works at a minimum level of integration.

Deliverables

The following products are the outputs of this phase:

Baselined software product

Unit tests

Unit test results

Function integration tests

Function integration test results

System-level test cases

Exit Criteria

This phase is complete when the following have been reviewed and, in those instances identified by an *, brought under configuration control:

Baselined software product*

Unit test, unit test results (optional under configuration control)

Function integration tests, function integration test results (as needed)

Product documentation

System-level test case description*—signature V.P. engineering, product manager, quality assurance manager

Description

During this phase the software product design is implemented and the various modules that make up the software are tested at the unit and functional level and then integrated into a system. In addition, the system test cases will be created (having already been described and defined in previous phases) and the "alpha" draft of the product documentation is created and distributed for review.

Step 1. Code and Unit Tests

Purpose:	Implement the software design and prove that the modules created fulfill the functionality of their design
Inputs:	Software design document
Team:	Primary—development engineers
	Secondary—software quality assurance, development leads
Tasks:	1. Implement software design
	2. Perform code walk-throughs (steps 3 and 4 could be executed before step 2)
	3. Create unit tests
	4. Run unit tests
	5. Fix bugs
	6. Turn over to configuration control (optional)
	a. code modules
	b. unit tests
	c. unit test results
References:	Coding standards, design methodologies, tools
Exit criteria:	When all units have been developed and meet with the approval of the engineering lead

Step 2. Functional Integration Tests

Purpose: To group individual software modules together so that they represent clearly identifiable functions that fulfill implementation requirements or act in support to implementation requirements. These functional groups of modules can then be pieced together and tested as a system, by the developers, prior to formal system-level testing.

Inputs: Software design specification, software modules

Team: Primary—development engineers
          Secondary—software quality assurance

Tasks: 1. Link units that make up a function
           2. Create function-level test cases
           3. Run function-level test cases
           4. Build a system from functions
           5. Test the functions as a system
           6. Submit software modules to configuration control

References: N/A

Exit criteria: When the project manager authorizes submittal of software modules to configuration control for baseline control

Step 3. Create System Test Cases

Purpose:	To create the individual system-level test cases based on the previous descriptions
Inputs:	System test plan, software requirements specification, product documentation
Team:	Primary—software quality assurance
	Secondary—product team (e.g., development engineering, marketing, application evaluation)
Tasks:	1. Review system test plan, software requirements specification
	2. For each test case "populate" or create data for
	a. Hardware/software configuration and preset conditions
	b. Inputs
	c. Expected outputs
	d. Test procedures
	e. Assumptions and constraints
	3. Issue test case
	4. Review, identify issues, resolve issues
References:	Attachment G—System Test Specification Template
Exit criteria:	This step is complete when the system test case definitions have been approved and submitted to configuration control

Phase Five: System Test

Purpose

Provide management with reliable information concerning the degree to which the software meets its functional and performance requirements.

Deliverables

The following products are the outputs of this phase:

    System test results

    System test reports

    Updated Software Design Document

    Baselined product

Exit Criteria

This phase is complete when the software product has passed all system-level tests and the Software Design Document reflects the "as built" design of the product.

Description

During this phase the software product is tested to ensure that the product meets the customer requirements. Tests are executed to prove functionality, performance, and reliability. Errors found in the product are fixed by development engineering and the tests are rerun. This level of testing can be performed from several to several dozen times.

Step 1. Execute System Test Cases

Purpose:	To determine the degree to which the software product conforms to its functional and performance requirements
Inputs:	System test plan, system test specification, product documentation, baselined software
Team:	Primary—software quality assurance
	Secondary—development engineering, technical publications
Tasks:	1. Install software product on system test hardware
	2. Execute each test case
	3. Issue test report
	4. Review test report with development engineering
	5. Update test cases and product (if necessary)
	6. Repeat steps 1 through 5
	7. Update the Software Design Document created in step 2 of Phase three
References:	Attachment G—System Test Specification Template
Exit criteria:	This step is complete when the software product has passed all system-level tests or management has determined to exit this phase

Phase Six: Product Evaluation

Purpose

To evaluate the product from a user's viewpoint in order to determine the product's usability.

Deliverables

The following products are the outputs of this phase:

    Alpha Evaluation Report

    Beta Evaluation Report

    Updated product baseline

Exit Criteria

This phase is complete when the product (both software and documentation) has been evaluated according to the evaluation goals identified in the alpha evaluation plan or by mutual agreement between engineering and marketing management.

Description

During this phase application engineers will evaluate the product from the user's perspective. Problems found by the application engineer will be reported to engineering. Engineering will attempt to fix the problems or identify a work-around. Engineering will deliver an updated version of the product to the application engineers for further evaluation when marketing management determines that its organization is prepared to test the updated version. Once a product is through alpha evaluation it will be shipped to the beta sites. Engineers will respond to beta sites with help messages and phone fixes. At the end of the beta period fixes are applied to any problems discovered during beta and the product is baselined in preparation for release to manufacturing.

Step 1. Alpha Evaluation

Purpose:	To make an in-house, user's view of the product in order to determine the product's usability in regard to functionality, performance, and ease of use
Inputs:	System tested product baseline, user documentation, known error list and work-arounds, alpha evaluation plan
Team:	Primary—application engineers
	Secondary—software quality assurance, engineering
Tasks:	1. Evaluate the product's functions against criteria as established in alpha evaluation plan
	2. Evaluate the product's characteristics against criteria established in alpha evaluation plan
	3. Submit problem reports against product problems
	4. Continue applications evaluation until the entire alpha evaluation suite has been run or until marketing determines the need for a new baseline to test against
	5. Engineering delivers a new baseline (incorporating fixes or work-arounds to previously reported problem reports)
	6. Repeat steps 1 through 5 until alpha evaluation is complete or the evaluation is terminated
	7. Submit evaluation reports
References:	Attachment I—Alpha Evaluation Plan
Exit criteria:	This step is complete when marketing management has determined that the goals of the alpha evaluation plan have been met or when management terminates the evaluation effort

Step 2. Beta Evaluation

Purpose:	To evaluate the product in a user environment to determine the product's quality in regard to functionality, performance, testability, and ease of use
Inputs:	Software baseline, user documentation, known error list and work-arounds, beta plan
Team:	Primary—marketing
	Secondary—development engineering, software quality assurance
Tasks:	1. Assemble beta product for beta release
	2. Perform inspection of beta product
	3. Ship beta product
	4. Perform site preparation activities according to beta plan
	5. Manage beta evaluation (unless managed by purchaser)
	6. Support remote and on-site beta evaluation activities
	7. Provide fixes or work-arounds to beta-discovered software reports
	8. Review weekly beta reports
	9. Review Final Beta Summary Report
References:	Attachment J—Beta Evaluation Plan
Exit criteria:	This step is complete when marketing has determined that the goals of the beta evaluation plan have been met or when supplier or purchaser management terminates the evaluation effort

Phase Seven: Product Release

Purpose

To ensure that the product masters delivered to the production vendor represent the product baseline and to assure that the production versions reflect the product baseline.

Deliverables

The output of this phase is the product prepared for shipment to the purchaser.

Exit Criteria

This phase is complete when the product has been shipped.

Description

During this phase software quality assurance works with document control and quality control to ensure that the product delivered to the purchaser represents the software production baseline. Through a series of quality assurance checks and signoffs the product is manufactured (replicated), boxed, and shipped to the customer.

Step 1. Release to Manufacturing

Purpose: To identify, baseline, and deliver the contents of the product to the manufacturer

Inputs: Software product, Version Description Document, and directory listing

Team: Primary—configuration management, document control

Secondary—software quality assurance, product marketing, engineering

Tasks: 1. Create Version Description Document

2. Print out product directories

3. Match the product directories to Version Description Document

4. Deliver master product to vendor or replication (if performed by third party)

5. Check vendors directory contents and against supplier's products directories

6. Order production quantities

References: Attachment K—Version Description Document

Exit criteria: This step is complete when production quantities have been ordered

Step 2. Release to Customer

Purpose:	To identify, baseline, and deliver the contents of the product to the customer
Inputs:	Version Description Document and directory listing
Team:	Primary—configuration management and document control
	Secondary—software quality assurance, product marketing, engineering
Tasks:	1. Inspect product against Version Description Document
	2. Release for shipment
References:	Attachment K—Version Description Document
Exit criteria:	This step is complete when the software product has been shipped to the customer

Phase Eight: Maintenance

Product enhancements require at least a tailored version of the SPH based on the size and complexity of the enhancement. Bug fixes should follow the basic change process described in the section on configuration management.

Attachment A: Marketing Requirements Template (or Customer Requirements Document)

1. Product overview

    (a) Description

    (b) Strategic purpose

    (c) Problems this product will solve

2. Assumptions and risks

3. Scope

    (a) System context chart

    (b) Product context chart

        1. Inputs
        2. Outputs

4. Functional capabilities

    (a) Inputs, outputs, brief description

    (b) States (assuming this is a new product where the customer knows this information and in-house engineering does not)

        1. State definition
        2. Behavior within each state
        3. Moving from one state to another

5. Customer/user description

6. Operational use

    (a) Which functions are used most often, under what conditions

    (b) Rank functions by criticality

7. Configuration/compatibility

    (a) Hardware

    (b) Prior releases of same product

    (c) Current company products

    (d) Third-party products

8. Technical constraints

    (a) Timing

    (b) Memory

(c) Throughput

(d) Security

(e) Audibility

(f) Agency/industry standards

(g) Internationalization

9. Analysis of product

 (a) Range of applicability

 (b) Originality in design and implementation

 (c) Volatility of requirements

 (d) Others

   1. Hardware exists/does not exist
   2. Real-time processing
   3. Interface to third-party software exists/does not exist

10. Quality and reliability goals

11. User documentation requirements

12. Productizing, installation, bundling

13. Future features

14. Reference documents

 (a) Specifications

 (b) Third-party documents

 (c) Marketing plan

15. Preliminary development cost and schedule

16. Appendices

Attachment B: Marketing-Engineering Interface During the Creation of the Marketing Requirements Document (MRD)

The Marketing Requirement Document, which represents the purchaser requirements, serves as input to the creation, by engineering, of preliminary costs and schedules. The MRD also serves as the baseline from which the software requirements specification is created. Even though the preliminary costs and schedules are estimates, it is important to make them as quickly and accurately as possible since they will dictate whether the organization commits resources to the development effort and what functionality the product will contain. Therefore, the more explicit and detailed the MRD is, the better the estimates and the quicker the turnaround in creating the software requirements specification. Here is an approach that will allow marketing and engineering to support each other in the creation of the MRD.

The inputs to the MRD effort are customer interviews, surveys, sales reports, marketing analysis, etc. Based on this input, marketing has to identify the key customer requirements to be implemented in terms that can be understood by engineering. Much of the information needed by engineering can be filled out in a straightforward manner. During this initial development phase a member, or members, of engineering is assigned to help marketing fill in those sections that marketing believes engineering can help with. This engineer can access the knowledge of other engineers during this effort. At the same time the engineer is reviewing the other sections to help with consistency issues, depth of detail, and identifying features that could be added as well as those that are at most risk.

Once a draft MRD has been created and received tentative approval within the marketing organization, the draft can be presented to a small group of engineering managers. An example of this group would be the engineering director, project manager, and project technical lead. This meeting is an informal walk-through of the MRD where the marketing and engineering authors explain the document to the audience. Questions at this point are meant to address format and clarification as opposed to detailed content questions.

Once agreed-upon changes to the MRD have been made, it is ready for general distribution and review. Comments are due back to the engineering project manager 24 hours in advance of any formal review of the MRD. The comments are given to the marketing author who should review them before the formal review.

After the formal MRD review and agreed-upon changes have been made, engineering must create a preliminary estimate and schedule. This can be done by addressing each of the marketing requirements and giving a rough estimate in lines of code or engineering hours. These estimates will be based on prior experience with similar products, best engineering judgments, and industry averages. If the estimates are given in lines of code that number can be divided by a number between 3 and 6 (depending on the application and portion of application) to arrive at engineering. Given the total number of hours required engineering can match that number against the total number of hours available. If there are fewer hours available than required, engineering can work with marketing to determine which marketing requirements can be modified or dropped. In addition, marketing and engineering can support each other in a request for reallocation of organizational resources in order to meet those marketing requirements for which engineering lacks the resources to develop. If there are more hours available to engineering, then future features could be moved up to the proposed next release.

Attachment C: Software Requirements Specification Template

1.0 Product overview

    1.1 Description

    1.2 Strategic purpose

    1.3 Problems this product will solve

2.0 Assumptions and risks

3.0 Scope

    3.1 System context chart

    3.2 Product context chart

        a. inputs
        b. outputs

4.0 Implementation requirements

    4.1 MRD capability X

        4.1.1 Implementation requirement X

            a. what it does[1]
            b. how does it start
            c. inputs/outputs
            d. error handling
            e. problem report fixes

        4.1.2 Implementation requirement XX

            a. what it does
            b. how does it start
            c. inputs/outputs
            d. error handling
            e. problem report fixes

    4.2 MRD capability XX

        4.2.1 Implementation requirement X

            a. what it does
            b. how does it start
            c. inputs/outputs

---

[1]A through e represent a recommended format for describing each implementation requirement.

        d. error handling

        e. problem report fixes

   4.2.2 Implementation requirement XX

        a. what it does

        b. how does it start

        c. inputs/outputs

        d. error handling

        e. problem report fixes

4.3 MRD capability XX

   4.3.1 Implementation requirement X

        a. what it does

        b. how does it start

        c. inputs/outputs

        d. error handling

        e. problem report fixes

   4.3.2 Implementation requirement XX

        a. what it does

        b. how does it start

        c. inputs/outputs

        d. error handling

        e. problem report fixes

5.0 Derived requirements

   5.1.1 Derived requirement

        a. what it does

        b. how does it start

        c. inputs/outputs

        d. error handling

   5.1.2 Derived requirement

        a. what it does

        b. how does it start

        c. inputs/outputs

        d. error handling

6.0 Requirements state table/design flow: The system being developed may be state driven; therefore, certain requirements may exist in one or more states

7.0 Technical constraints: Identify how the technical constraints identified in the MRD (e.g., timing, sizing, throughput) will affect any of the implementation or derived requirements

8.0 Users operations: A general discussion of what the user operations are, the information needed to perform the operation, and general error handling to be performed

    8.1 Operation 1

        a. description

        b. information needed

        c. command line entries

        d. error handling

    8.2 Operation 2

        a. description

        b. information needed

        c. command line entries

        d. error handling

9.0 Platforms supported

10.0 Compatibility

    10.1 Prior releases of same product

    10.2 Current company products

    10.3 Third-party products

11.0 Detailed data definitions

    11.1 External interfaces (cite references)

    11.2 Interfunctional requirement

    11.3 Platform specific data

12.0 Testing

    12.1 Special testing/certification

    12.2 Qualification matrix

	Demonstration	Analysis	Inspection
I1			
I2			
I3			
I4			

13.0 Requirements traceability matrix

14.0 Reference documents

   14.1 Specifications

   14.2 Third-party documents

   14.3 Marketing plan

15.0 Attachments

   (a) Preliminary user interface windows

Attachment D: Project Development Plan

1. System overview: Briefly state the purpose of the system

2. Product deliverables

3. Activity schedule and milestones (e.g., design, code, test)

    (a) When does it start
    (b) When does it end
    (c) What does it produce
    (d) Sequential relationship to other activities

4. Training plan

5. Resources

    (a) Hardware
    (b) Software
    (c) Facilities

6. Risks

    (a) What are they
    (b) How will you monitor them
    (c) What will you do if they occur

7. Reviews

8. Interface with contractors

    (a) Reference to contractor statement of work
    (b) Reference to contractor plans
    (c) Identification of reviews and action item processing

9. Detailed estimates for each phase

10. Statusing and reporting methods

Attachment E: Software Design Document Template

1. High-level product description (copied from MRD)

2. Engineering assumptions and risks as applied to design

    2.1 Description

    2.2 Cause

    2.3 Solution

        a. person assigned

        b. date

3. Reference documents

    3.1 Specifications

    3.2 Third-party documents

    3.3 Standards

4. Scope (copied from software requirements specification)

    4.1 System context chart (where the product fits in the entire system)

    4.2 Product context chart

        a. inputs and description

        b. outputs and description

5. Software architectural design

    5.1 Program A

        5.1.1 inputs

            a. data

            b. control

        5.1.2 processing

        5.1.3 outputs

    5.2 Program N

        5.2.1 inputs

            a. data

            b. control

        5.2.2 processing

        5.2.3 outputs

6. Error processing design

    6.1 Sources and categories of errors

6.2 Error detection

6.3 Error processing

7. Database design

    7.1 Object identification

        7.1.1 Object 1

           a. name

           b. attributes

        7.1.2 Object N

           a. name

           b. attributes

    7.2 Database schema

        7.2.1 File 1

           a. name

           b. object

           c. keys

        7.2.1 File 2

           a. name

           b. object

           c. keys

    7.3 Database transaction descriptions

        7.3.1 Transaction 1

        7.3.2 Transaction 2

8. Software detail design

    8.1 Program A

        8.1.1 Module 1

           a. inputs

               1. data

               2. control

           b. processing

           c. outputs

        8.1.1 Module N

           a. inputs

               1. data

               2. control

           b. processing

           c. outputs

8.2 Program N

    8.2.1 Module A

        a. inputs

            1. data

            2. control

        b. processing

        c. outputs

9. Error handling traceability matrix

10. User interface screens and windows

    10.1 Functional windows

    10.2 Supporting windows

11. Requirements traceability matrix

Attachment F: System Test Specification Template

1. High-level product description (copied from MRD)

2. Assumptions

3. Risks

    3.1 Description

    3.2 Cause

    3.3 Solution

        a. Person assigned

        b. Date

4. Scope of testing

    4.1 What will be tested

    4.2 What will not be tested (and why)

    4.3 What percentage of code will be tested

5. Costs and schedules

    5.1 Training

    5.2 Create test cases

    5.3 Execute test cases

6. Test environment

    6.1 Software requirements

    6.2 Hardware requirements

    6.3 Installation requirements

7. Test case description

    7.1 Test name

    7.2 Test objective

    7.3 Qualification method

    7.4 Assumptions and constraints

    7.5 Type of data to be recorded

8. Verification requirements traceability matrix

9. Reference documents

    9.1 Specifications

    9.2 Third-party documents

    9.3 Standards

Attachment G: System Test Specification Template

1. High-level product description (copied from MRD)

2. Scope

   2.1 What will be tested

   2.2 What will not be tested

3. General setup

   3.1 Installation

   3.2 Data recording

   3.3 Environment variable settings

   3.4 Test file backup, naming, and version control procedures

4. Test case definition

   4.1 Test case name

   4.2 Test objective

   4.3 Hardware/software configuration

   4.4 Materials

   4.5 Setup

   4.6 Inputs

   4.7 Expected outputs

   4.8 Test procedures

   4.9 Test results file name

5. Verification requirements traceability matrix

6. Test report form

   6.1 Test name

   6.2 Test engineer

   6.3 Date and time of test

   6.4 Product begin tested (hardware and software configuration)

   6.5 Name and location of

       a. test inputs
       b. test outputs
       c. expected outputs
       d. test log

6.6 Test results

    a. Deviation from baselined test procedures

    b. Identification of test step that failed

    c. Identification of problem reports opened

    d. Remarks

7. Reference documents

    7.1 Specifications

    7.2 Third-party documents

    7.3 Standards

Attachment H: Documentation Plan Template

1. Product overview

    a. Description

    b. Strategic purpose

    c. Problems this product will solve

2. Assumptions and risks

3. Documents to be created

    a. Name

    b. Purpose

4. Documents to be modified

5. Audience profile

6. Design implications

7. Media selection

8. Estimated costs and schedules

9. Appendices

Attachment I: Alpha Evaluation Plan

1. Product being evaluated

   1.1 Name

   1.2 Version

2. Scope of evaluation

3. Assumptions

4. Entrance criteria to alpha evaluation

   4.1 List of functional requirements tested in system test

   4.2 System test results

   4.3 List of known bugs and their work-arounds

5. Resources required (in addition to that already available to alpha evaluation)

   5.1 Hardware

      a. What
      b. When
      c. How long

   5.2 Software

      a. What
      b. When
      c. How long

   5.3 Evaluation engineers

      a. Who
      b. When
      c. How long

6. External (to alpha evaluation) dependencies

   6.1 Documentation

   6.2 People

   6.3 Products

7. Schedule and budget

   7.1 Major tasks (begin/end dates)

   7.2 Hours required per task

8. Functions to be evaluated

   8.1 Inputs

   8.2 Outputs

   8.3 Method of grading

9. Functions not evaluated (and why)

10. Features

   10.1 Performance

   10.2 Usability

   10.3 Recoverability

   10.4 Installability

   10.5 User documentation

11. Evaluation report template

   11.1 Report number

   11.2 Function(s)/features evaluated

   11.3 Evaluator

   11.4 Date/time

   11.5 Preset conditions

   11.6 Results (e.g., ease of use, limitations, etc.)

   11.7 Positive comments

   11.8 Areas for needed improvement

   11.9 Problem reports

      a. Fix before beta
      b. Fix after beta

   11.10 Evaluator's summary

Attachment J: Beta Evaluation Plan

1. Goals

   1.1 Duration

   1.2 General goals

2. Assumptions

3. Beta sites selected

   3.1 Type A (managed by supplier)

      3.1.1 Why chosen

      3.1.2 What do they get

      3.1.3 Begin and end date for evaluation

      3.1.4 Managed/unmanaged

      3.1.5 Number of sites

   3.2 Type B (Managed by purchaser)

      3.2.1 Why chosen

      3.2.2 What do they get

      3.2.3 Begin and end date for evaluation

      3.2.4 Managed/unmanaged

      3.2.5 Number of sites

4. What is to be tested and at what site (possibly a matrix)

   4.1 Portability

   4.2 Performance

   4.3 Reliability

   4.4 Usability

   4.5 Support levels

   4.6 Ease of installation

   4.7 Compliance with standards

   4.8 Documentation

   4.9 Design flows

5. Supplier resources to support beta

   5.1 On-site

   5.2 At supplier site

6. Pre Installation:

   6.1 Type A

      6.1.1 Site preparation

      6.1.2 Security

      6.1.3 Site checklist[2]

      6.1.4 Feedback system

   6.2 Type B

      6.2.1 Site preparation

      6.2.2 Security

      6.2.3 Site checklist

      6.2.4 Feedback system

7. Weekly engineering report on beta effort

8. Entry criteria to production

9. Final beta summary report: an overview of the beta test where analysis of the beta tests results is performed with the intention of determining how well marketing's product goals were met as well as the supplier's performance of the beta effort

   Installation support: Customer and developer perceptions of how well the installation was supported.

   Start-up problems: Specific issues and fixes during beta testing.

   Documentation: End-user response to documentation provided with the product. Include any upgrades performed or suggested for the future.

   Manpower: Staffing issues that may have influenced the beta test process. Indicate whether the product has been sufficiently exercises.

   Review of problem reports and prioritize fixes/work-arounds/signoffs of any problem reports.

   Other: Miscellaneous.

---

[2]Site-specific implementation checklist. A site-specific checklist should be prepared and completed before beta testing. Compiling the checklist is primarily a marketing responsibility but engineering may be called upon to resolve problems. The checklist may include, but is not limited to, site configuration control board requirement, installation specific data, product design/flow specific information, etc.

Attachment K: Version Description Document

    I. System overview: Brief description of the system

    II. Version description: Brief description to include number and date

    III. Physical materials (listings, tapes, disks, documentation, etc.)

    IV. Software modules by name, date, version

    V. Enhancements

    VI. Bug fixes

    VII. Configuration settings

    VIII. Versions of supplier and third-party interface compatibility

    IX. Installation and bring-up instructions and tests

    X. Known problems and suggested work-arounds

Further Readings

Beizer, Boris. 1983. *Software Testing Techniques*. Van Nostrand Reinhold, New York, N.Y.

Hetzel, Bill. 1988. *The Complete Guide to Software Testing*. QED Information Sciences, Inc., Wellesley, Mass.

Humphrey, Watts S. *Managing the Software Process*. Addison-Wesley, Reading, Mass.

Jones, Capers. 1991. *Applied Software Measurement*. McGraw-Hill, New York, N.Y.

Myers, Glenford. 1979. *The Art of Software Testing*. Wiley Interscience, New York, N.Y.

Index